I0711834

Peace Begins *in the* Womb

*Reflections from a
Pro-Life Feminist*

Marilyn Kopp

authorHOUSE

AuthorHouse™
1663 Liberty Drive
Bloomington, IN 47403
www.authorhouse.com
Phone: 833-262-8899

Published by AuthorHouse 05/02/2023

ISBN: 979-8-8230-0725-2 (sc)
ISBN: 979-8-8230-0724-5 (e)

Library of Congress Control Number: 2023908102

Print information available on the last page.

To my loving husband, Paul,
and to our kids,
Brittany, Emily, and Willy

CONTENTS

INTRODUCTION

I have always been pro-life. Growing up, I asked my mother what abortion was, and she told me. Thinking that it happened only with a terminal diagnosis, I said, "The baby's going to die anyway, right?" When she said no, I was shocked. I couldn't believe any woman could ever do that.

It wasn't until I became pregnant with my oldest daughter and felt her kicking that I decided I had to become an activist.

I found Feminists for Life (FFL) through my local Right to Life group. When I learned that the founders of the American feminist movement were pro-life, I knew I had found a home. (My articles and letters documenting the pro-life position of the early feminists can be found in the index under "feminist history.") I joined the Ohio FFL chapter in 1989 and became their communications director. From there, I went on to become president of the state chapter for ten years. I've been involved in advocacy ever since, including speaking engagements at many colleges and universities.

With the Supreme Court's historic *Dobbs v. Jackson Women's Health Organization* ruling on June 24, 2022, overturning *Roe v. Wade* and *Planned Parenthood v. Casey*, the abortion landscape in this country was dramatically altered. The legality of abortion is now up to individual states to decide. Now more than ever, FFL's mission statement is particularly relevant: "Feminists for Life is dedicated to systematically eliminating the root causes that drive women to abortion—primarily, the lack of practical resources and support—through holistic, woman-centered solutions. Women deserve better than abortion."

This book is a collection of writings I've had published throughout the years, in reverse chronological order, along with articles and summaries of articles about FFL. The writings explore how abortion is inconsistent with authentic feminist values of justice, nonviolence and nondiscrimination. There are recurring phrases in my writing, but the concepts they express need to be reinforced. Each article or letter to the editor is numbered, and the index that follows them breaks them down into different areas of interest.

Minor editing has been done on these letters and articles. The goal is to correct any misspellings, punctuation, or grammatical errors in transcribing them. There has been no change in the meaning of any letter or article. Nothing substantive has been added or subtracted. Thank you to the newspapers for their help on copyright issues.

Thanks also to Angela Ferritto, John Luciano, Louis H. Pumphrey, Elizabeth Shoemaker, and Joseph P. Meissner for their assistance. Finally, thanks to FFL president Serrin M. Foster for her support for this project and for allowing me to use the FFL slogan, "Peace Begins in the Womb," as a title to this book.

If you, the reader, are pro-life, I hope you find the book helpful in articulating a pro-woman, pro-life perspective on the abortion issue. If you are pro-choice, I hope you find the pro-life feminist perspective to be an interesting and challenging one that results in many substantive conversations. Finally, I hope this book leads us all to realize that we really aren't so far apart after all.

PART 1

Published Articles and Letters to the Editor

This section includes my writings, reprinted with permission, exploring the concept of pro-life feminism.

1

Pregnant Women Need Support, Not a Killing Option

In response to the May 15 articles about abortion, "A look at the state laws restricting abortion rights" and "Cincinnati suburb's abortion ban is challenged in court": women have a right to control their bodies. But when a woman is pregnant, there is clearly a separate body growing in her womb. It's unjust to treat that body as property to be violently disposed of, in the same way it was unjust for women to once be treated as property of their husbands.

Regarding the May 15 photos of the abortion rights rally in downtown Cleveland that drew more than a thousand people: "What is right is not always popular and what is popular is not always right."

Abortion doesn't liberate women. It merely enables them in adopting the same unjust standards as their oppressors. Pregnant people need resources and support, not killing, to solve their problems.

MARILYN KOPP
Cleveland

The writer is a member of Feminists for Life.

The Plain Dealer
Wednesday, May 18, 2022

2

In Reality, Abortion Has Made Women Less Equal

In his December 1 commentary, "Overturning *Roe v. Wade* would tear the country apart," Eugene Robinson claims that *Roe* recognizes that "the Constitution protects a woman's freedom over her own body." But a woman's "own body" doesn't have two heads, four arms, and four legs. There is clearly a genetically separate body involved in every abortion.

Robinson states that, with *Roe*, "the nation took a giant stride toward treating women as full and equal citizens under the law." To the contrary, *Roe* set up the male reproductive experience as the model for economic and social success. In order to achieve equality, women must change their bodies to become like men, wombless and unpregnant at will.

This has set back accommodation of pregnancy and motherhood in the workplace and in other areas of society. Abortion pits mother against child and uses lethal violence to do so. It's time to correct this grievous injustice and restore peace in the womb.

Marilyn Kopp, Cleveland
The writer is a member of Feminists for Life.

The Plain Dealer
Wednesday, December 8, 2021

3

Deaths from Illegal Abortions before Roe Are Overstated

Regarding the October 9 letter "*Roe v. Wade* prevented deaths from unsafe, illegal abortions": the Centers for Disease Control and Prevention (CDC) began collecting data on abortion mortality in 1972, the year before *Roe v. Wade* was decided. Seventeen states had liberalized abortion laws prior to *Roe*, the *Washington Post* reports.

In 1972 the number of US deaths from legal abortions was twenty-four, and from illegal abortions, thirty-nine, according to the CDC. Although even one death is too many, it's a far cry from the thousands per year that abortion-rights proponents like to claim.

Studies show that most illegal abortions were not performed by so-called back-alley butchers but by physicians who simply chose to break the law. Dr. Mary Calderone, president of Planned Parenthood, wrote in 1960 that participants in a 1955 conference "estimated that 90 percent of all illegal abortions are presently being done by physicians."

Furthermore, legal abortion is not the "safe" procedure it's made out to be. Complications are common and underreported, including potentially fatal uterine perforations, lacerations, blood loss, infections, blood clots, and other complications.

Today, thousands of pregnancy care centers offer alternatives to abortion, which empower mothers to choose life for themselves and their children.

Marilyn Kopp, Cleveland
The writer is a member of Feminists for Life.

The Plain Dealer
Sunday, October 24, 2021

4

Loss of a Life Is Too High a Price for Women's Gains

Regarding Christine Garapic's September 7 letter, "Shame on justices for letting abortion law stand": I agree that it is hypocritical for legislators to oppose abortion while also using the "freedom of choice" argument to oppose COVID-19 safety measures such as mandating face masks and vaccinations to protect human life.

Garapic states that she is "strongly an advocate of a woman's right to choose what happens to her body." Yet in every pregnancy, there is clearly a separate human body growing and developing that deserves protection.

When our liberation costs innocent human lives, it is merely oppression redistributed to the unborn child. Women deserve resources and support to empower them to make life-affirming choices for themselves and their children.

Using killing to solve social problems is unjust. Women deserve better than the violence of abortion.

Marilyn Kopp, Cleveland
The writer is a member of Feminists for Life.

The Plain Dealer
Friday, September 10, 2021

5

Commentary from the Community—
The Upcoming Care for Her Bill Would
Help Support New Mothers

By Marilyn Kopp

US Representative Jeff Fortenberry of Nebraska is working on soon-to-be-introduced legislation called "Care for Her." This bill seeks to meet the emotional, physical, social, financial, and other needs that a woman encounters during pregnancy, childbirth, and child-rearing by facilitating support and services.

Feminists for Life has worked extensively to advocate and organize support for pregnant and parenting women on college campuses and in the workplace, as well as for poor and other vulnerable pregnant and parenting women. After three decades of groundbreaking work in these areas, we know from listening to women that more is needed. Care for Her can make a crucial difference.

Most women don't really want abortions; it's something that women with unplanned pregnancies often feel they need because they have no other choices. As former FFL vice president Frederica Mathewes-Green has pointed out, "No woman wants an abortion like she wants an ice cream cone or a Porsche. She wants an abortion as an animal caught in a trap wants to gnaw off its own leg." It's an act of desperation and self-loss, and the self-evident sentiment expressed in this quote has made it a favorite among pro-choice women as well.

As a member of FFL, I had the honor of serving on the national steering committee for the Common Ground

Network for Life and Choice in Washington, DC, for three years.

The Care for Her bill takes no position on abortion and is a prime example of coming together around the most pressing issues pregnant and parenting women face in school, at work, and in society. It can be supported by both pro-choicers and pro-lifers and by people of all political parties.

The bill provides a pregnancy child tax credit for expecting mothers of $3,600, which they need and deserve, just as they do once their babies are born.

The legislation also proposes practical support for pregnant and parenting women, including federal grants to assist with health care and maternal support; mentorship and parenting resources during pregnancy and following the birth of a child; opportunities for completion of education, employment, and job training; and safe, affordable housing during pregnancy.

Furthermore, this act would also establish a new federal-state entity that evaluates and organizes all available resources and programs that a pregnant woman qualifies for. Each state that participates would provide expectant mothers with a list of those resources, assuring her that the community is prepared to nurture and support both her and her child. In addition, the bill would establish a new incentive of supplemental funds to communities that demonstrate improved maternal and child health outcomes.

Fortenberry explained in an interview in FFL's biannual magazine, *The American Feminist*, that Care for Her "lets a woman know that we, as a community of care, will be there through the miraculous journey of giving life."

In a June 23 piece for the *Washington Post*, columnist Henry Olsen wrote, "This bill makes a firm national commitment to a comprehensive support structure for pregnant women, which has been lacking despite many specific programs. Over time, this structure can be built into a robust and nurturing environment so that no pregnant woman fears she will face motherhood alone."

FFL's mission statement recognizes that "Abortion is a reflection that our society has failed to meet the needs of women. We are dedicated to systemically eliminating the root causes that drive a woman to abortion—primarily lack of practical resources and support—through holistic, women-centered solutions. Women deserve better than abortion."

Care for Her goes a long way toward achieving that goal. I urge our US representatives from Ohio to demonstrate their commitment to women by supporting Care for Her.

Kopp is a past president of Feminists for Life of Ohio, serving for 10 years. She also worked for the city of Cleveland for 31 years in engineering and in cartography and has three grown children.

The Plain Dealer
Friday, July 23, 2021

Note: The Care for Her bill is on hold, as Jeff Fortenberry is no longer a member of Congress.

6

Worthiness Underlies Debate about Abortion

Regarding the April 14 article "Divided court upholds law banning Down syndrome abortions":

In an August 6, 2018, paper, "Biologists' Consensus on 'When Life Begins,'" Steven Andrew Jacobs of the University of Chicago's Department of Comparative Human Development cited a survey in which 95 percent of biologists "affirmed the biological view that a human's life begins at fertilization."

The abortion conflict centers not so much on when life begins as when that life is protectable, when that life has enough worth to be considered a member of the human community, a "person." Should there be two classes of human beings under the law—persons with the right not to be killed and nonpersons, human beings, without this right? There are waiting lists of couples wanting to adopt Down syndrome babies, if the mother so chooses. Abortion dynamites the foundation of feminism and poisons the well against civil rights for the disabled and other vulnerable populations.

Marilyn Kopp, Cleveland
The writer is a member of Feminists for Life.

The Plain Dealer
Friday, April 30, 2021

Taking a Life Will Not Solve Social Problems

Regarding Jack Topeka's March 5 letter supporting the death penalty ("Letting murderers avoid execution isn't justice"): Killing someone to show them that killing is wrong makes no sense. We learn early in life that two wrongs never make a right.

Topeka asked how we can justify spending his tax dollars to feed and house criminals who murder. Studies have shown that the appeals process and other expenses related to the death penalty are more costly than life in prison without parole.

We must teach our children and set by example that all human life has dignity and value. In a truly civilized society, we don't treat people as property to be disposed of, whether it's the prisoner on death row, the child in the womb, or assisted suicide for the elderly that is little different from legalized euthanasia.

It's unjust to use killing as a solution to social problems. We are better than that.

Marilyn Kopp, Cleveland
The writer is a member of Feminists for Life.

The Plain Dealer
Tuesday, March 9, 2021

8

Promote Life-Affirming Alternatives to Abortion

Friday will mark the 48th anniversary of the controversial *Roe v. Wade* Supreme Court decision that legalized abortion nationwide. Tragically, according to the Guttmacher Institute, there were approximately 862,320 abortions performed in the United States in 2017 alone.

Pregnancy reflects the beauty, power, and strength of a woman's body. But for those who can't conceive and for women with unplanned pregnancies, adoption is a life-affirming option.

According to Ryan Hanlon, vice president of the National Council for Adoption, "There are many thousands of families waiting to be matched through adoption with a newborn." Clearly there are loving homes for babies at risk for abortion.

There are even waiting lists for couples wanting to adopt babies with special needs, including Down syndrome or spina bifida. Furthermore, if more babies were placed into loving adoptive homes, we'd have fewer children ending up in foster care.

Using the lethal violence of abortion as a solution to social problems is unjust. Let's encourage women with life-affirming resources, support, and alternatives such as adoption so that ours can be truly called a culture of life.

Marilyn Kopp, Cleveland

The Plain Dealer
Tuesday, January 19, 2021

9

Abortion Begins as an Injustice Against Women

In her Nov. 22 letter, "Pro-choice women need an advocate right now," Charlotte Biller wrote that many pro-choice women "face being forced to bear children against their will."

Once a woman becomes pregnant, she is already bearing a child. The only way to change that is to either give live birth or to kill the child that is already growing in her womb.

Abortion is an injustice against fetal life that begins with injustice against female life. It's unjust to force a woman to choose between her life goals and her own child instead of providing her with the resources and support she needs to carry her pregnancy to term.

Using lethal violence to kill a woman's unborn child is not liberation but simply oppression redistributed.

I am a member of Feminists for Life.

Marilyn Kopp, Cleveland

The Plain Dealer
Sunday, December 6, 2020

Roe v. Wade: Not the "Equality" Women Should Be Seeking

Many people fear *Roe v. Wade* will be overturned by a conservative majority on the Supreme Court. They view abortion as an essential part of women's equality.

But instead of liberating women, abortion has liberated men from obligations to their partners and children. When women say, "It's my body, my right, my choice," men hear, "Then it's your problem."

We have long wanted men to be more involved in child-rearing—to be more than just breadwinners and disciplinarians—yet we shut them out of any say in the abortion decision.

Sex has consequences, one of which is creating a new, unique human life. Women's equality is not found by imitating irresponsible men who are free to walk away from unplanned pregnancies and 18 years of child support through abortion.

Rather, it's found by demanding equal care and shared nurturing of lives unintentionally conceived.

At the same time, we need to work together to ensure pregnant women have the nonviolent, life-affirming resources and support they need to carry their pregnancies to term. We must do better than using killing as a solution to our social problems.

Marilyn Kopp, Cleveland

The Plain Dealer
Sunday, November 1, 2020

11

Let's Work Together to Make Abortion Unthinkable

Regarding the June 30 article, "Ruling strikes down Louisiana abortion law":

The Supreme Court decided 5–4 to overrule a Louisiana law requiring abortionists to have admitting privileges at a hospital within 30 miles of the abortion facility. In Louisiana, all other ambulatory surgical centers have this safety requirement. Abortionists should be held to the same standards.

But regardless of which way the court ruled, it's time we stopped telling women they can't finish school or follow their dreams without abortion. Life-affirming alternatives, resources, and support are available for any woman facing an unplanned pregnancy at thousands of pregnancy care centers nationwide. We need to let more women know about these free services that help both during and after pregnancy. No woman should be forced to choose between her future and her own child.

As Destiny Herndon-De La Rosa, founder of New Wave Feminists, stated, "We need a cultural shift in consciousness that sees the humanity of both the unborn child and the mother, and works to protect and serve both equally."

Let's work together to make abortion unthinkable.

Marilyn Kopp. Cleveland

The Plain Dealer
Tuesday, July 7, 2020

12

Pro-life Attitude over Virus Should Extend to Abortions

According to an April poll by Baldwin Wallace University's Community Research Initiative, the vast majority of Ohioans supported Gov. Mike DeWine's stay-at-home order and other restrictions put in place to combat the coronavirus ("Ohio likes DeWine more than Trump," April 27).

In other words, most of us were willing to dramatically curtail and restrict our personal bodily autonomy in order to save other, more vulnerable lives. As the death toll from COVID-19 rises, we know that each fatality represents the loss of a unique, valuable, irreplaceable human being.

This logic should also extend to abortion and protecting vulnerable human life in the womb.

When we use freedom of bodily autonomy to endanger the lives of others, we run the risk of devaluing all human life—something we see happening all too often in our culture today. You cannot put a price on the value of human life.

Marilyn Kopp, Cleveland

The Plain Dealer
Tuesday, May 12, 2020

13

Abortions Are Contrary to State Orders during Pandemic

Regarding the March 31 article "Federal judge blocks Ohio from using coronavirus health order to restrict abortions":

Abortion clinics need to adhere to the same order by Ohio Health Department Director Dr. Amy Acton that every other provider must follow: to cease all elective surgeries so that enough protective equipment is available for health-care workers fighting the COVID-19 pandemic.

Furthermore, abortion is not medicine, because pregnancy is not a disease. The right to control your body should not include the right to destroy somebody else's.

The bigger question we must ask ourselves is what is wrong in society that causes a woman to feel such desperation that she sees taking her own child's life as an "essential" and viable action. There are life-affirming options (such as those found at pregnancy resource centers) we must avail ourselves of that preserve life, rather than take it.

Marilyn Kopp, Cleveland

The Plain Dealer
Tuesday, April 7, 2020

14

Let's Promote Culture of Life with Roe v. Wade Anniversary

Jan. 22 marks the 47th anniversary of the Supreme Court's controversial ruling in the *Roe v. Wade* decision, which legalized abortion nationwide. Those who defend abortion like to frame opposition to it as a "war against women." Yet women lead most of the national pro-life organizations. Also, various polls have shown that men support more liberal abortion laws than women do.

According to a January 2017 Marist Poll on abortion, the overwhelming majority of women want abortion restricted and don't want it funded by tax dollars. A majority also think that, regardless of its legality, abortion is morally wrong and that it causes more harm than good to women in the long run.

The poll also found the vast majority of women think it's possible to have laws that protect both the health and well-being of a woman and the life of the unborn instead of it being necessary for laws to protect one and not the other. This *Roe* anniversary, let's resolve to seek life-affirming solutions to the problems faced by women with unplanned pregnancies so that ours can truly be called a culture of life.

Marilyn Kopp, Cleveland
The writer is a member of Feminists for Life.

The Plain Dealer
Sunday, January 19, 2020

15

Instead of Abortion, Consider Having Your Baby Adopted

Thank you for your uplifting Dec. 8 article, "Adoption reunion resonates with many." In 2015, Ohio law changed, opening birth records for individuals adopted between 1964 and 1996, allowing many of these individuals to seek reunions with their birth parents.

Open adoption can be a loving and life-affirming option for women facing an unplanned pregnancy.

According to the Adoption Network Law Center, there are approximately 1 million to 2 million couples waiting to adopt. For every baby adopted, there are up to 36 couples waiting.

The Guttmacher Institute reported that approximately 862,320 abortions were performed in the United States in 2017. Only 4% of women with unplanned pregnancies place their children through adoption, according to the Adoption Network Law Center.

If more babies were placed in loving, adoptive homes, instead of being aborted or raised by unprepared parents, there would eventually be fewer children ending up in the foster care system.

There are even waiting lists for people wanting to adopt babies with special needs. In the abortion decision, there's no such thing as an "unwanted" child.

Marilyn Kopp, Cleveland
The writer is a member of Feminists for Life.

The Plain Dealer
Monday, December 16, 2019

16

Give Pregnant Women What They Need for Life-Affirming Choices

In the Oct. 2 article "Ohio abortions down 2%," the Ohio Department of Health reported the number of abortions performed in our state dropped by 2% from the year before and hit an all-time low since statistics were first kept in 1976.

It's unclear why there are fewer abortions, but experts have said better contraception, fewer unintended pregnancies, and state restrictions may play a role. This is good news.

Abortion is a symptom of, not a solution to, the continuing struggles women face in the workplace, on campus, at home, and in the world at large. Instead of seeking ways to increase abortion access, we can promote nonviolent alternatives, such as those offered at pregnancy care centers. No woman should feel forced to choose between her education or career plans and her own child.

By giving pregnant women the resources and support they deserve to make life-affirming choices, we'll help restore a cultural respect for human life that seems to be lacking in our society today.

Marilyn Kopp, Cleveland
The writer is a member of Feminists for Life.

The Plain Dealer
Friday, October 11, 2019

17

You Really Need to See "Unplanned"

The controversial movie "Unplanned" recently opened in theaters nationwide. It's a powerful and compelling film based on the true story of Abby Johnson, former Planned Parenthood abortion clinic director who later became a pro-life activist.

Once named as a Planned Parenthood "Employee of the Year," and the youngest woman to direct a clinic, Abby had a profound change of heart after guiding an ultrasound probe during a 13-week-gestation abortion in her Texas clinic. Abby watched in horror as the baby on the screen desperately twisted away from the intrusive suction catheter being inserted into the woman's uterus. When the suction machine is turned on, the baby is dismembered, disappearing slowly from the screen.

The film's writers-directors Chuck Konzelman and Cary Solomon defended this disturbing scene as being faithful to Abby's personal account and said it had been vetted by Anthony Levatino, a retired obstetrician-gynecologist and former abortionist who plays the doctor in the scene.

The movie was given an "R" rating not for sex, drugs, or profanity, but for violence. A 16 year old can have an abortion, but she can't see a film about it without being accompanied by a parent or guardian.

The movie flashes back to the beginning of Abby's eight-year involvement with Planned Parenthood as a college student who was recruited at school to volunteer as a clinic escort. She undergoes two abortions herself, one surgical and another chemical, with the use of the abortion drug RU-486. Abby is told by clinic staff that she would experience cramping and bleeding like a heavy period. After suffering at home through

12 hours of hemorrhaging and excruciating pain, she finally falls asleep on the bathroom floor covered with blood. The cramping lasted eight weeks.

As clinic director, Abby is told by her superiors that the clinic must double its quota of abortions performed. She was reprimanded for insubordination by expressing her opinion that the new quota policy conflicted with Planned Parenthood's mission statement. After the reprimand, and after witnessing the traumatic ultrasound-guided abortion, she retreats to a nearby pro-life advocacy center and decides to resign from Planned Parenthood. Abby goes on to form "And Then There Were None," a nonprofit organization that has helped 500 people leave the abortion industry. The group reports that after watching the film, an additional 94 workers have contacted them asking for help getting out of their jobs.

Abby's conversion is strikingly similar to that of former abortion doctor Bernard Nathanson. He once ran the largest abortion clinic in the US and was a co-founder of the National Association to Repeal Abortion Laws, which later became NARAL Pro-Choice America. He was instrumental in legalizing abortion. Like Abby, he changed his mind after watching an ultrasound of an abortion and later narrated a well-known documentary about it called "The Silent Scream."

Abortion defenders often cite the "hundreds of thousands" of women who died of illegal abortions before *Roe v. Wade*. In his 1979 book "Aborting America," Dr. Nathanson refuted that figure. He wrote, "It was always '5000 to 10,000 deaths a year.' I confess that I knew the figures were totally false … but in the 'morality' of our revolution, it was a useful figure, widely accepted, so why go out of our way to correct it with honest statistics?"

As expected, Planned Parenthood, the nation's largest abortion provider, issued a statement about "Unplanned," saying "The movie promotes many falsehoods including most importantly, distortions and incorrect depictions about health care." This denial is not surprising; Planned Parenthood performs 911 abortions a day and takes in $127 million in profits annually. After its release, the film was the fourth top-grossing movie in the country, despite the fact that several TV networks refused to air its trailer and its Twitter promotional account was temporarily suspended on opening weekend for no clear reason.

As the film demonstrates, instead of empowering and liberating women, abortion more closely reflects patriarchal values: seeking power through control and domination, condoning violence on the grounds of personal privacy, and using killing as a solution to conflict.

Viewers should definitely see this important film and decide for themselves.

Marilyn Kopp is a past president of Feminists for Life of Ohio.

Marilyn Kopp
The Washington Examiner
Thursday, April 25, 2019

18

Eliminating the Root Causes of Abortion

March is Women's History Month. As we honor the brave women who marched before us, let us keep in mind that their messages provide us with a clear vision of where we need to go. Perhaps on no other issue is that more important than abortion. Because modern feminism is so closely associated with abortion rights, few know that the founders of the women's movement believed in the worth of all human life and strongly opposed abortion.

The same women who fought for the rights of women to vote also fought for the unborn to be born and for their mothers to be supported.

Our foremothers didn't oppose abortion merely because the procedure was less safe at the time. While they were certainly concerned with maternal health, the terminology they used for abortion—"child murder," "infanticide," "a degrading and disgusting crime"—indicates a concern for the safety of the other individual involved as well. They did not retract their opposition even after the introduction of sterile techniques made the procedure much safer.

Nor were they slaves to the prudish notions of sex in their Victorian era. Many were advocates of the concept of "free love." Elizabeth Cady Stanton wrote that "a healthy woman has as much passion as a man."

The early feminists were pioneers in expanding women's roles in society, but they didn't believe it should come at the expense of their unborn children. They believed abortion was a symptom of women's oppression, not a solution to it. Mattie Brinkerhoff wrote in 1869, "When a man steals to satisfy hunger, we may safely conclude that there is something wrong in society—so when a woman destroys the life of her unborn child, it is an evidence that either by education or circumstances she has been greatly wronged."

Like Susan B. Anthony and the other early American suffragists, today's pro-life feminists envision a better world in which no woman would be driven by desperation to abortion. As Anthony once stated, "Sweeter even than to have had the joy of caring for children of my own has it been to me to help bring about a better state of things for mothers generally, so their unborn little ones could not be willed away from them."

Groups such as Feminists for Life are dedicated to systemically eliminating the root causes that drive women to abortion, primarily the lack of practical resources and support, through holistic, women-centered solutions. For nonviolent, empowering, and life-affirming alternatives to abortion, go to FFL's website or contact your local pregnancy care center for assistance.

FFL believes we must continue working toward a world in which pregnancy, motherhood, and birth motherhood are accepted and supported. We need college campuses and workplaces that support mothers in practical ways and do not force them to choose between their education or career plans and their own children. Let's foster a society that supports the role of mothers, values the role of fathers, and helps parents provide both financial and emotional support for their children.

Instead of advocating for unrestricted abortion-on-demand throughout all nine months of pregnancy and beyond, such as we're seeing in legislation out of the state of New York and several other states, pro-life feminists are working on ways to make it easier for pregnant women to choose life for themselves and their unborn children. We can do that by fighting pregnancy discrimination in the workplace, advocating for more quality and affordable child care, better maternity leaves, flex time, job sharing, telecommuting, shared parental responsibility, and enforceable child support.

On college campuses, FFL is working for affordable housing for students and their babies, financial aid and scholarship security, maternity coverage in student healthcare plans, flexible class scheduling, and counseling services for parenting and adoption.

Let us work to fulfill our foremothers' dream of a just society, free from violence and oppression, where women can reach their greatest potential and where the lives and rights of all are honored and valued. Abortion will never fulfill that dream, but by working together, we can make abortion unthinkable.

Marilyn Kopp is past president of the Ohio chapter of Feminists for Life.

Marilyn Kopp
The Washington Examiner
Tuesday, March 26, 2019

19

Listen to Women's Day Founders

I find it ironic that pro-choice groups chose Aug. 26, Women's Equality Day, to protest the nomination of Brett Kavanaugh to the Supreme Court because they fear it will lead to overturning *Roe v. Wade.* Women's Equality Day commemorates the passage of the 19th Amendment in 1920, granting women the right to vote. But what NARAL Pro-Choice America fails to acknowledge is that the women who fought for the right to vote were adamantly and unanimously opposed to abortion.

In Susan B. Anthony and Elizabeth Cady Stanton's radical feminist newspaper, *The Revolution,* abortion was condemned as "child murder," a "most degrading and disgusting crime," and "infanticide." They saw it as an injustice against fetal life that begins with injustice against female life.

This Woman's Equality Day, let's honor them by listening to them.

Marilyn Kopp
Cleveland

The Plain Dealer
Sunday, August 19, 2018

20

Abortion Is Part of Women's Oppression

I was saddened by the May 27 article "Irish measure on abortion rights wins soundly," an outcome that will lead to legal abortion in that country. Oral O'Connor stated, "This is about women's equality" and is "a rejection of an Ireland that treated women as second-class citizens."

Unleashing lethal violence against the weakest and most vulnerable members of the human family is not progressive and liberates no one. How can women ever lose second-class status as long as they are seen as requiring surgery to avoid it? Nature didn't make women inferior, and it's an injustice to say we must change our biology to participate freely and equally in society.

Legal or not, abortion is a symptom of women's oppression, not a solution to it. Instead of offering the life-affirming resources and support that pregnant women deserve, society is let off the hook with a harsh and destructive solution to the "problem" of an unintended pregnancy.

If we truly valued women, we wouldn't force them to choose between sacrificing their life plans and dreams or undergoing a humiliating procedure that destroys their own child—a choice men aren't forced to make. Women deserve better.

Marilyn Kopp
Cleveland

The Plain Dealer
Wednesday, June 20, 2018

21

Let's Empower Women with Resources

In her article ("Ohio's abortion restrictions disproportionally impact rural women," *Forum*, April 25), Reilly Wieland dismisses abortion restrictions as being "politically motivated." This contradicts what many opinion polls say, including a 2017 Marist Poll that found the overwhelming majority of women in this country want abortion restricted. It also found a majority of women think abortion is morally wrong and that it causes more harm than good to women in the long run.

Wieland said, "Science … should guide how abortion is provided, not politics." Although the fetus grows in a woman's body, science tells us it has its own body, separate DNA, heartbeat and brain waves and is a totally unique genetic creation. We have long ago rejected the idea that women are the property of men. Now we are passing the same kind of oppression down on our vulnerable unborn children, disposing of them as we see fit and calling it liberation.

Instead of working to expand access to abortion, we should be working to make it unthinkable by addressing the root causes and by empowering women with life-affirming, nonviolent resources and support.

Marilyn Kopp
Cleveland

The Plain Dealer
Sunday, May 6, 2018

Refuse to Choose. Women Deserve Better.

Monday is the 45ᵗʰ anniversary of the *Roe v. Wade* Supreme Court decision that legalized abortion in the United States. More than 50 million lost lives later, debate on the issue remains as polarized as ever.

All too often women don't abort out of freedom of choice, but rather out of a sense they have no other choices. As author Frederica Mathewes-Green wrote, "No woman wants an abortion like she wants an ice cream cone or a Porsche. She wants an abortion like an animal caught in a trap wants to gnaw off its own leg." It's an act of desperation and loss.

While most women know how to get an abortion, fewer are aware of resources and support available to empower them to keep both mother's and child's lives and bodies intact. Search for local pregnancy care centers such as Womankind or go to Feminists for Life's site, Women Deserve Better, for help.

This *Roe* anniversary, let's work together to make abortion unthinkable by facilitating life-affirming, nonlethal alternatives that promote dignity and respect for all. Refuse to choose. Women deserve better.

Marilyn Kopp
Cleveland

The Plain Dealer
Sunday, January 21, 2018

23

The Original Feminism Is Pro-life

Jan. 22 is the 45th anniversary of the *Roe v. Wade* Supreme Court decision that legalized abortion in the United States. That's 45 years and more than 60 million yet-to-be-born children being legally terminated by their parents.

Looking at modern feminism, we see that instead of its early emphasis on the rights of women to equal pay and equal votes, it has been narrowed to a defense of abortion rights. Feminists who oppose abortion are often drowned out of conversation with their pro-abortion-rights sisters. The result is that few people are aware that the founders of the women's movement were, without known exception, opposed to abortion. These activists saw it as a symptom of women's oppression, not a solution to it. Today's pro-life feminists agree. Here are a few examples of the early feminists' stance on abortion:

* Mattie Brinkerhoff (1869): "When a man steals to satisfy hunger, we may safely conclude that there is something wrong in society—so when a woman destroys the life of her unborn child, it is an evidence that either by education or circumstances she has been greatly wronged."

* Victoria Woodhull (1875): "Men must no longer insult all womanhood by saying that freedom means the degradation of women. Every woman knows that if she were free, she would never bear an unwished-for child, nor think of murdering one before its birth."

* Susan B. Anthony (c. 1870s): "Sweeter even than to have had the joy of caring for children of my own has it been to me to bring about a better state of things for mothers generally, so their unborn little ones could not be willed away from them."

Our feminist foremothers didn't oppose abortion because it was less safe at the time. While they were certainly concerned for women's health, their terminology for abortion included phrases like "child murder," "infanticide," and "ante-natal murder," which indicated a concern for the other individual involved as well.

Today's pro-life feminists are active as advocates for both women and their children, born and unborn. For example, Feminists for Life holds that abortion violates authentic feminist principles of justice, nonviolence, and nondiscrimination.

Feminists for Life maintains that abortion rather reflects traditional patriarchal values: seeking power through control and domination, condoning violence on the grounds of personal privacy, and using killing as a solution to conflict. These views represent a renaissance of the original American feminism. Like the early American suffragists, today's pro-life feminists envision a better world in which no woman would be driven by desperation to abortion.

It is unjust to ask a woman to choose between sacrificing her life plans or her own child in order to participate freely and equally in society. Instead, let us work together to systemically eliminate the root causes that drive women to abortion—primarily lack of practical resources and support—through holistic, woman-centered solutions. For instance, across the United States there are more pregnancy care centers that assist pregnant women and new mothers than there are abortion clinics. These centers offer life-affirming choices and practical help through alternatives such as paternal child support, adoption options, referrals for child care and employment, and pre- and postnatal medical services. Abortion clinics, like those of Planned Parenthood, the nation's largest abortion provider, offer few if any such services.

Feminists for Life has led the revolution on campuses

through their College Outreach Program, striving to meet the needs of college-aged women, the demographic that has the highest rate of abortion. Since the group's College Outreach Program began in 1994, there has been a dramatic 30 percent decrease in abortions among college-educated women.

There are also numerous solutions to be found at FFL's website, www.womendeservebetter.com. Women do deserve better than abortion.

This *Roe* anniversary, refuse to choose. Peace begins, after all, in the womb.

Marilyn Kopp is past president of Feminists for Life of Ohio.

Marilyn Kopp
The Washington Examiner
Friday, January 19, 2018

24

Saturday Is Women's Equality Day

Women's Equality Day is Saturday, when we celebrate the passage of the 19th Amendment in 1920 giving United States women the right to vote.

It's commonly believed feminism is deeply rooted in abortion rights. Therefore, it's important to note that, without known exception, the women who bravely fought for the right to vote also fought for the rights of unborn children to be born and for their mothers to be supported.

Our feminist foremothers recognized abortion is a symptom of women's oppression, not a solution to it. Asking women to choose between sacrificing their life plans or their own children in order to participate freely and equally in society is unjust.

In the words of suffragist leader Susan B. Anthony, "Sweeter even then to have had the joy of caring for children of my own has it been to me to help bring about a better state of things for mothers generally, so their unborn little ones could not be willed away from them."

Let's learn from their wisdom. Let's continue their work to address the root causes that drive women to abortion by empowering them with nonviolent choices regarding their bodies and lives.

Marilyn Kopp
Cleveland

The Plain Dealer
Friday, August 25, 2017

25

There Are Alternatives to Abortion

Many Cleveland-area residents have noticed several billboards put up recently by an abortion clinic stating, "I'm grateful for my abortion." This clinic performs abortions through the 20th week of pregnancy, the legal limit in Ohio. In response, Feminists for Life (FFL) has installed four new "Peace Begins in the Womb" billboards, starting on June 8, for four weeks.

FFL's entire billboard fundraising campaign came not from grants, corporate donors, or government funding, but rather from grassroots organizing. We are feminists who believe in nonviolent, empowering choices for women and their children. Our voices are strong in declaring that "peace begins in the womb."

Feminists for Life of America recognizes that abortion is a reflection that our society has failed to meet the needs of women. We are dedicated to systemically eliminating the root causes that drive women to abortion—primarily lack of practical resources and support—through holistic, women-centered solutions.

If you or someone you know is pregnant or parenting and needs help, contact us at feministsforlife.org. There are life-affirming alternatives to abortion that don't involve killing. We are pro-nonviolent choice. Women deserve better than abortion.

I am FFL's billboard project coordinator.

Marilyn Kopp
Cleveland

The Plain Dealer
Sunday, June 18, 2017

26

Nonviolent Alternatives to Abortion

Regarding "Preterm weathers the legislative storm," (Letters, Jan. 30): Instead of helping women to violently dismember their own children in the womb, we need to empower women with life-affirming, constructive solutions to unplanned pregnancies.

Abortion is a reflection that our society has failed to meet the needs of women. We at Feminists for Life are dedicated to eliminating the root causes that drive women to abortion—primarily a lack of practical resources and support—through holistic, woman-centered solutions.

A report by Planned Parenthood's former research arm, the Guttmacher Institute, reveals that since FFL began our College Outreach Program in 1994, abortions among college-educated women have decreased 30 percent.

Ohio has more pregnancy resource centers to assist pregnant women and new mothers than it has abortion clinics. These centers offer practical help with paternal child support, adoption options, referrals for child care and employment, and pre- and postnatal medical services.

Abortion violates authentic feminist principles of justice, nonviolence, and nondiscrimination. Women deserve better.

Marilyn Kopp
Cleveland

The Plain Dealer
Sunday, February 5, 2017

27

Mother Against Child—Mortal Enemies

Regarding "Years go by, but women will still head out of state for their needs," (Forum, Dec. 16): Connie Schultz picks the worst stereotypes of pro-lifers to represent those who supported the recently signed legislation in Ohio banning abortions after 20 weeks of pregnancy. She states, "Right-wing extremists who support laws such as this are driven by an insatiable desire to shame women. They want us to feel dirty and immoral and unworthy in the eyes of God as they define him."

This dismissive generalization of pro-lifers is insulting to the many thousands of Ohio women who support this legislation to protect unborn children at a relatively advanced stage of development.

Pitting women against their own children as mortal enemies is an injustice that can be perpetrated only in a society that oppresses women instead of liberating them. That attitude is reflective of patriarchal values that condone violence on the grounds of personal privacy and use killing as a solution to conflict.

Women deserve better than abortion. Refuse to choose between mother and child—we can love them both—and acknowledge the loss of those who have made this tragic choice.

Marilyn Kopp
Cleveland

The Plain Dealer
Wednesday, December 28, 2016

28

Women's Rights and Abortion 'Rights' Do Not Mix: Marilyn Kopp (Opinion)

Aug. 26 is Women's Equality Day, which commemorates the passage of the 19th Amendment to the US Constitution in 1920 granting women the right to vote. Another landmark anniversary in women's history is Jan. 22, 1973, when the Supreme Court's *Roe v. Wade* decision legalized abortion in the United States.

Many contemporary feminists consider abortion to be an integral part of women's rights. As such, they are unaware that the same women who fought for the right to vote also fought for the rights of the unborn to be born and for their mothers to be supported. It's important to understand the suffragists' adamant opposition to abortion as we continue the fight for equal rights today.

Our feminist foremothers recognized abortion as a symptom of women's oppression, not a solution to it. In 1869, Mattie Brinkerhoff wrote, "When a man steals to satisfy hunger, we may safely conclude that there is something wrong in society—so when a woman destroys the life of her unborn child, it is an evidence that either by education or circumstances she has been greatly wronged."

They also recognized that abortion is an injustice against fetal life that begins with injustice against female life. "Men must no longer insult all womanhood by saying that freedom means the degradation of woman. Every woman knows that if she were free, she would never bear an unwished-for child, nor think of murdering one before its birth," wrote free love advocate and first woman presidential candidate Victoria Woodhull in 1875.

Abortion was classified as "child murder," on the same level as infanticide, in the radical feminist newspaper *The Revolution*, published by Susan B. Anthony and Elizabeth Cady Stanton. *The Revolution* refused to accept paid advertisements from patent medicines, because they were thinly disguised abortifacients. Such ads were a major source of income for women's periodicals at the time, and the loss of that revenue in part contributed to driving *The Revolution* into bankruptcy.

Today, most women do not abort out of freedom of choice, but out of a desperate sense that they have no other choices. It is unjust today, as it was a century ago, for women to feel forced to choose between their life plans and their own children in order to participate freely and equally in society. Our feminist foremothers' insights on abortion and women's rights are still relevant—and badly needed—in today's divisive debate. This is not slavishly adhering to tradition, but rather creating a firm understanding of where we have come from in order for us to have a clear vision of where we need to go.

According to a recent report by the Guttmacher Institute, college-aged women 20 to 24 years old continue to be the highest risk group for having abortions.

More than 20 years ago, Feminists for Life initiated a College Outreach Program to provide assistance to pregnant and parenting students on campuses nationwide. We involve students, faculty, and administrators in identifying support such as housing for parents and their babies, child care, telecommuting options, and maternity coverage in student health care plans.

How can we honestly say women have freedom of choice without access to any of these resources?

In addition, there are more pregnancy care centers

nationwide that offer free support for those facing an unplanned pregnancy than there are abortion clinics. These centers provide assistance with social services, pre- and postnatal medical care, adoption counseling, housing, and referrals for employment and child care. We need to make women aware of these options. We need to encourage support and nonviolent solutions to problem pregnancies in order to achieve consistent justice and true equality.

We can resolve to work together to end this tragic social experiment on women and children and make abortion unthinkable by offering life-affirming alternatives. Peace begins, after all, in the womb.

Guest Columnist/cleveland.com
Sunday, August 21, 2016

Marilyn Kopp of Cleveland served for ten years as president of the Ohio chapter of Feminists for Life of America.

29

There's No Plight Abortion Can Solve

The US Supreme Court ruled in an abortion facility medical-standards case to strike down Texas's laws that restrict abortion clinics and protect women's health and safety ("Justices strike Texas abortion clinic limits," June 28).

Justice Stephen Breyer said that the law would have created an obstacle for women seeking abortions.

What Breyer fails to acknowledge is that women are driven to abortion because of obstacles they face in their lives. And now, the court has put abortion providers' interests above those of women.

Hillary Clinton stated, "Women won't be punished for exercising their basic rights."

But children are not punishment. Having someone reach up inside you with a sharp instrument to dismember your child can be more reasonably viewed as punishment.

Many women turn to abortion out of desperation because they are concerned about their financial situations or about a lack of support from family, an employer or school, or the father of the child.

Abortion is not a solution. Empty arms and empty wombs do not solve her problems.

The abortion debate will continue until we embrace constructive rather than destructive alternatives for problem pregnancies that don't involve killing.

Marilyn Kopp
Cleveland

Kopp is a member of Feminists for Life.

The Plain Dealer
Saturday, July 9, 2016

30

'Pro-life' Covers a Lot of Ground

"Primary season has sundered GOP relations with evangelicals" (Forum, May 15) presents opposition to abortion as a key position of the religious right. It should be noted that although religious conservatives make up one element of the pro-life movement, they are hardly the only ones.

Consider the Consistent Life Network—more than 200 organizations and several hundred individuals committed, according to its mission statement, "to the protection of life, which is threatened in today's world by war, abortion, poverty, racism, capital punishment and euthanasia." Members believe that "these issues are linked under a consistent ethic of life."

Endorsers include diverse organizations and individuals such as Feminists for Life, the Pro-Life Alliance of Gays and Lesbians, Vegans for Life, Agnostics for Life, actor Martin Sheen, and Sister Helen Prejean, the author of *Dead Man Walking*.

The Consistent Life Network "challenges those working on all or some of these issues to maintain a cooperative spirit of peace, reconciliation, and respect in protecting the unprotected."

Marilyn Kopp
Cleveland

Kopp is a member of Feminists for Life.

The Plain Dealer
Monday, May 23, 2016

44

31

Early Feminists Opposed Abortion

March is Women's History Month. As we assess our progress, let's keep in mind that, without a complete understanding of where we've come from, it's harder to envision where we need to go. Perhaps on no other issue is that more true than abortion.

Because modern feminism is so closely associated with a defense of abortion rights, few realize that the founders of the women's movement believed in the worth of all human life and strongly opposed abortion.

The same women who fought for the rights of slaves to be free and the rights of women to vote also fought for the unborn to be born and for their mothers to be supported.

The early feminists viewed abortion as a symptom of women's oppression, not a solution to it.

Let's work to fulfill our foremothers' dreams of a just society, free from violence and oppression, where women can reach their greatest potential and where the lives and rights of all are honored and valued. Abortion will never fulfill that dream, but by working together, we all can.

Marilyn Kopp
Cleveland

Kopp is a member of Feminists for Life.

The Plain Dealer
Monday, March 21, 2016

32

Keep Babies' and Moms' Lives Intact

Today marks 43 years since the Supreme Court's *Roe v. Wade* decision legalized abortion in the United States, but the debate still rages on: Is abortion a woman's right or a terrible wrong against her? As things stand today, the answer is both.

Few would disagree that most women don't skip happily to the abortion clinic to dismember their unborn children. Rather, it is a difficult decision many women make because they feel they have no other choices.

We can do more to let pregnant women know they are not alone. Free assistance and support are available at many pregnancy resource centers. These life-affirming alternatives can empower women to keep both mother's and child's lives and bodies intact.

Marilyn Kopp
Cleveland

Kopp is a member of Feminists for Life.

The Plain Dealer
Friday, January 22, 2016

Choices Women Shouldn't Have to Make

It's unfortunate that Hillary Clinton and her supporters have adopted defense of abortion as an integral part of women's rights ("Clinton kicks Trump, outlines policies," Sept. 11). Conversely, it can be argued that abortion conflicts with authentic feminist principles of justice, nonviolence, and nondiscrimination.

The abortion mentality that decrees, "It's a baby if I want it; it's a fetus if I don't," reflects the ultimate intolerance. When we base any individual's worth on our emotional reaction to them, we are rationalizing prejudice.

It's unjust to make women choose whether to sacrifice their life plans or their offspring. It's not a choice women should feel compelled to make in order to participate freely and equally in society.

As the first woman to run for president, Victoria Woodhull, wrote in 1875, "Men must no longer insult all womanhood by saying that freedom means the degradation of woman. Every woman knows that if she were free, she would never bear an unwished-for child, nor think of murdering one before its birth."

Refuse to choose. There are life-affirming alternatives at pregnancy resource centers that don't involve killing.

Marilyn Kopp
Cleveland

Kopp is a member of Feminists for Life.

The Plain Dealer
Friday, September 25, 2015

Women Deserve Better than Abortion

Regarding the July 29 article "Move to cut funding is picking up momentum": Planned Parenthood is the largest abortion provider in the United States. State Rep. Kathleen Clyde stated efforts to defund the organization "clearly show the GOP's disrespect of women." Clyde disregarded that a substantial number of pro-lifers are, in fact, women.

Stephanie Kight, president and CEO of Planned Parenthood Advocates of Ohio, stated, "We have been and will continue to be there with compassionate care. Dismembering a woman's unborn child is not compassionate care." Abortion, in fact, more clearly reflects patriarchal values: condoning violence on the grounds of personal privacy and using killing to resolve conflict.

As the great feminist leader Elizabeth Cady Stanton wrote in 1873, "When we consider that women are treated as property, it is degrading to women that we should treat our children as property to be disposed of as we wish." *

We can work together to provide life-affirming alternatives that keep both mothers' and children's lives and bodies intact. Women deserve better than abortion.

Marilyn Kopp
Cleveland

Kopp is a member of Feminists for Life.

The Plain Dealer
Wednesday, August 5, 2015

Please note: This quote by Elizabeth Cady Stanton was originally found by an early Feminists for Life researcher in an October 16, 1875, letter to Julia Ward Howe in Howe's diary. It was believed to be at the Houghton Library at Harvard University. Later on, we understand that Harvard separated all the inserted documents from all the diaries. The letter can no longer be found. Some say it never existed, but it could very well have been lost, stolen, or destroyed. Regardless, Feminists for Life of America no longer cites this quote because it can't be proven.

35

The First Feminists Abhorred Abortion

March is Women's History Month. As it comes to a close, it's important to note the views of the suffragists and first-wave feminists who started the women's movement on one of the biggest issues of our day: abortion. Without exception, the founders of feminism believed in the worth of all human life and adamantly opposed abortion.

They were pioneers in expanding women's roles in society but didn't believe that expansion should come at the expense of unborn children. They believed abortion was a symptom of women's oppression, not a solution to it.

Our foremothers didn't oppose abortion because it was less safe at the time. Although they were concerned with maternal health, the terminology they used for abortion—"child-murder," "infanticide," "ante-natal murder"—indicates a concern for the safety of the other individual involved, as well.

Nor were they slaves to the prudish notions of sex in their Victorian era. Many were advocates of "free love." Elizabeth Cady Stanton wrote that "a healthy woman has as much passion as a man."

As we honor the brave women who came before us, let's pay them the ultimate compliment: Listen to them.

Marilyn Kopp
Cleveland

Kopp is a member of Feminists for Life.

The Plain Dealer
Sunday, March 29, 2015

36

Eliminate Root Causes of Abortion

Jan. 22 marks the 42nd anniversary of the *Roe v. Wade* Supreme Court decision, which legalized abortion in the United States.

Since 1973, pregnant women have felt compelled to sacrifice their own offspring with this tragic choice approximately 57 million times, according to the National Right to Life Committee. This estimate is based on data from the Guttmacher Institute (a former research arm of Planned Parenthood). Rather than serving as a symbol of liberation, abortion reflects a failure of society to meet the real needs of women.

On this *Roe* anniversary, let us dedicate ourselves to systematically eliminating the root causes that drive women to abortion—primarily a lack of practical resources and support. Let's make abortion unthinkable by facilitating holistic, life-affirming alternatives such as those offered by the many pregnancy resource centers in our communities and by college outreach programs. Women deserve better than abortion.

Marilyn Kopp
Cleveland

Kopp is a member of Feminists for Life.

The Plain Dealer
Friday, January 9, 2015

37

Better Choices than Abortion

Regarding Cynthia M. Allen's thoughtful essay, "New pro-choice movement message doesn't support or empower women," Oct. 1: All too often, women seek abortions out of desperation, because they feel they have no other choices.

Life-affirming options and free assistance can be found at more than 200 pregnancy care centers in Ohio.

As Allen points out, many women are still dealing with loss and regret after their abortion decisions. Many pregnancy centers provide postabortion counseling for healing and nonjudgmental support.

No woman should be forced to choose between sacrificing her life dreams or sacrificing her own child.

Refuse to choose. Women deserve better.

Marilyn Kopp
Cleveland

The Plain Dealer
Saturday, October 25, 2014

38

Hypocrisy on the Pro-choice Side, Too

In her Aug. 3 letter, "Pro-life argument stops at the border," Lyn Ziebro claims that Plan B (the morning-after pill) merely thins the uterine lining so a pregnancy does not implant. Therefore, she claims, it is not an abortion. That is not true. At least 10 medical dictionaries define pregnancy as beginning at conception and conception occurring at fertilization, not implantation. This definition can also be found in a number of embryology, obstetric, human anatomy or physiology textbooks.

It may be true, as Ziebro asserts, that pro-lifers who support the death penalty are hypocritical. But opponents of the death penalty who defend abortion are equally hypocritical. Contrary to public perception, studies in *Psychology Today* have shown pro-lifers are actually less likely to support the death penalty than pro-choicers are. This is not surprising. Many supporters of both capital punishment and abortion view certain life as dispensable if it's burdensome or inconvenient. Both seek to kill that which one can't control. Opposition to both reflects a more consistent life ethic.

Marilyn Kopp
Cleveland

Kopp is a member of Feminists for Life.

The Plain Dealer
Friday, July 8, 2014

39

Reproduction and Women's Rights: Abortion Contradicts the Very Values that Drove Feminist Fight for Equality

At the start of the US feminist movement 165 years ago, in Seneca Falls, NY, the "Declaration of Sentiments" was drafted with many demands. Yet the movement coalesced around one goal: securing the right to vote.

Women's Equality Day on Monday commemorated the achievement of that goal—after a 75-year battle—with the ratification of the 19th Amendment in 1920, granting political enfranchisement to women.

Fifty years ago a second wave of the women's movement was ignited by Betty Friedan's book *The Feminine Mystique*, which soon galvanized support behind another demand: legalized abortion. In assessing the impacts of these two legislative mandates in the fight for equal rights, some important distinctions bear noting.

Today abortion is usually considered the cornerstone of women's rights. Parallels are drawn between the antisuffragists and those today who want to deny women their "reproductive freedom" and keep them shackled to babies and the kitchen sink.

Thus, few today are aware that the founders of American feminism were staunchly and unanimously opposed to abortion. In Susan B. Anthony and Elizabeth Cady Stanton's radical feminist newspaper, *The Revolution*, abortion was condemned as "child murder," a "most degrading and disgusting crime," "ante-natal murder," and "infanticide."

Why would the original champions of women's equality

oppose such a fundamental "right"? The reason was the same for the abolitionists: Every individual, regardless of race or gender, is entitled to basic human rights and dignity, and those rights cannot be given or taken away by others.

Early feminists' pro-life views went well beyond the antiabortion rhetoric of their day. To eliminate the "evil" of abortion, they argued we must reach the root cause: society's oppression of women.

Victoria Woodhull, free-love advocate and first woman presidential candidate, wrote in 1875, "Every woman knows that if she were free, she would never bear an unwished-for child, nor think of murdering one before its birth." Abortion was recognized as a symptom of, not a solution to, women's oppression. They anticipated its elimination, not its wholesale acceptance.

In the 1960s, legitimate social problems were still preventing women from reaching their fullest potential: an unfair burden of child care, pay inequity, job discrimination, sexual harassment, domestic violence and a lack of legal and financial rights.

The right to vote was considered the "red herring of the revolution" because it did not alleviate these problems. Women just voted like their husbands with low poll turnout, and we still have far to go to reach parity in representation. The drive for legal abortion came in response to this lag.

While suffrage didn't achieve all the goals its proponents expected, it didn't detract from them either. Conversely, abortion directly contradicts the very values that drove the feminists' fight for equality. The emphasis on abortion has actually hindered progress toward real reform.

Instead of liberating women, abortion liberated men. Obligations to their partners and children are optional, with child abuse and the feminization of poverty escalating with the availability of abortion, and more of the child-care burden has shifted to women. Abortion, instead of social change that would facilitate combining children and career, has relieved society of its obligation to accommodate the real needs of women.

Pro-choice women have abandoned core feminist values and adopted the worst patriarchal standards: seeking power through control and domination, condoning violence on the grounds of personal privacy, and using killing to resolve conflict. By insisting on abortion as necessary for equality, we assume the traditional male worldview: equating personhood to manhood and denying women's reproductive capacities. Women must become essentially wombless and unpregnant like males and resort to violence to do so.

Let us reevaluate the causes around which we rally in order to achieve a more inclusive society. As we honor our brave foremothers, let us heed their wisdom. As abortion has not brought us closer to our goal, let us instead support causes that reflect true feminist ideals of justice and nonviolence. These will bring women the respect they deserve.

Kopp, a member of Feminists for Life, lives in Cleveland.

The Plain Dealer
Wednesday, August 28, 2013

Evaluating Portman's Shift on Gay Marriage: Some Pro-lifers Are Liberal

I object to your portrayal of all pro-lifers as conservatives in your June 9 article on Sen. Rob Portman. Opposition to abortion can also be argued from a liberal perspective, as witnessed by groups such as the Pro-life Alliance of Gays and Lesbians, Feminists for Life, and Democrats for Life.

Feminist support for abortion seems particularly ironic, considering that we long ago rejected the notions that women are the property of their husbands or that a woman's worth depends on her desirability to a man. It is hypocritical to impose the same unjust standards on children.

Pro-lifers are often painted as intolerant right-wingers. Yet the abortion mentality that decrees, "It's a baby if I want it; it's a fetus if I don't," reflects the ultimate intolerance. Giving voice to the voiceless has always been and should always be a priority of liberals.

Marilyn Kopp
Cleveland

Kopp is a member of Feminists for Life.

The Plain Dealer
Sunday, June 16, 2013

41

Forty Years after Roe v. Wade, the Issue Is Far from Settled

Jan. 22 marks the 40th anniversary of the *Roe v. Wade* Supreme Court decision, which legalized abortion in the United States.

"Safe, legal and rare" is a goal many pro-choicers advocate. But with 1,210,000 abortions a year in this country, it is hardly rare.

Women are deeply divided on the abortion issue. Both the pro-life and pro-choice sides attempt to offer a compassionate response to a complicated situation—but with different outcomes.

But as author Frederica Mathewes-Green writes, "Is this a woman's choice? What a horrible, bloody, humiliating choice. A woman who wants an abortion seems like an animal caught in a trap, trying to gnaw off its own leg—a terrible bid to escape a desperate situation by an act of violence and self-loss."

If we are concerned with sustaining and nurturing relationships, it seems too obvious that abortion severs and divides. Let us build on the support and resources that are already available by offering life-affirming alternatives so that no woman feels forced to choose between her life plans or her own child. On this *Roe* anniversary, let's work together to make abortion much more than illegal. Let's make it unthinkable.

Marilyn Kopp
Cleveland

Kopp is a member of Feminists for Life.

The Plain Dealer
Sunday, January 13, 2013

Sen. Turner's ED Bill Is Sad and Absurd

State Sen. Nina Turner's sarcastic introduction of a bill to restrict men's access to erectile dysfunction drugs in retaliation for the GOP lawmakers' anti-abortion bills (*Plain Dealer*, Thursday) is an absurd distortion of the abortion question into a silly his-body/her-body comparison. She assumes it is only men who are against abortion, while many women are as well, holding that abortion runs counter to true feminist ideals. Women are no longer their husbands' property, are they? Similarly, it is hypocritically unjust to consider women as "owners" of their children, to dispose of them as they see fit.

Apparently, Turner believes abortion is necessary for women's equal and free participation in society. Her sad joke about erectile dysfunction drugs serves only to belittle her argument. True reform that would advance women's legitimate goals would remove the oppression that forces them to alter their biology to match men's in order to be equal, to sacrifice their children lest they lose out on their dreams for education and careers. All the injustices that lead a woman to consider abortion must be corrected. The sooner we realize that, the better off women will be.

Marilyn Kopp
Cleveland

Kopp is a member of Feminists for Life.

The Plain Dealer
Monday, December 10, 2012

43

Contraception Mandate Spurs Mixed Reaction: Ladies, Refuse to Choose

In President Barack Obama's campaign ad on abortion ("Ad misrepresents Romney position," July 30), a woman states, "I've never felt this way before, but it's a scary time to be a woman.... We need to attack our problems, not a woman's choice."

I agree that we need to attack our problems, but in a constructive manner that looks at the prospective mother and child as partners, not a destructive manner that casts them as enemies. If a pregnant woman is so desperate that she sees the death of her own child as a possible option, then our society is truly regressive rather than progressive, rooted in a horrific social injustice.

How can an act of despair be referred to as a "choice"? Women can choose to sacrifice their life plans and dreams, or they can undergo a humiliating, invasive operation and have their own child die. It's a lousy choice that women should not be forced to make. Refuse to choose. We can keep both mother's and child's lives and bodies intact with life-affirming alternatives. Peace begins, after all, in the womb.

Marilyn Kopp
Cleveland

Kopp is a member of Feminists for Life.

The Plain Dealer
Sunday, August 5, 2012

44

Pregnancy Centers Help Moms, Babies

Thanks to Regina Brett for her column ("Babies already here need your help, too," Dec. 11) mentioning local pregnancy care centers that provide life-affirming alternatives to abortion. These centers deserve our support so that no woman feels forced to choose between sacrificing her life plans or sacrificing her own child. More assistance for women facing an unplanned pregnancy can be found in the Yellow Pages under "Abortion Alternatives" or by Googling "Abortion Alternatives in Cleveland, Ohio."

Brett suggested that we should do more to help babies who have already arrived in this world. Unfortunately, the availability of abortion has not reduced the incidence of child abuse or child poverty. Would anyone propose that "unwantedness" is so severe a problem as to warrant putting a 5-year-old to death? Why should that same child be put to death six years earlier?

We should address poverty by finding solutions to eradicate poverty, not to eradicate the children of poor people. We can support mothers. We can support babies both born and unborn. And we can solve problems without killing.

Marilyn Kopp
Cleveland

Kopp is a member of Feminists for Life.

The Plain Dealer
Sunday, December 18, 2011

45

Services for Women Who Choose Life

Thirty-seven years after *Roe v. Wade* legalized abortion, how much progress has been made? Women are still being forced to choose between sacrificing their life plans or sacrificing their offspring. Educating women about life-affirming alternatives to abortion is a goal we should all agree on.

The majority of pro-life volunteer work and resources goes directly into the provision of services for pregnant women and new mothers. Such services don't make the kind of headlines that advocacy does, but there are more pregnancy help centers nationwide than there are abortion clinics.

These centers provide practical assistance with reasonable child care, paternal child support, maternity or parental leave from work, good adoption options, continuing education, and pre- and postnatal medical services. They can be found in the Yellow Pages under "Abortion Alternatives."

We can keep both the mother's and the child's lives and bodies intact. Abortion reflects a failure to meet our real needs. Women deserve better.

Marilyn Kopp
Cleveland

Kopp is a member of Feminists for Life.

The Plain Dealer
Thursday, January 28, 2010

Abortion Weakens Civil Rights of Everyone

Hillary Clinton and Barack Obama were asked whether life begins at conception.

Clinton responded that the potential for life begins at conception, and Obama said he didn't know the answer.

In 1981, when the Senate held hearings on when life begins, the report concluded that the biological point of beginning (conception) was not in dispute. The conflict centers, instead, on when life is protectable.

Should there be two classes of human beings under the law: persons with the right not to be killed, and nonpersons, human beings, without this right?

If we put any living members of the species outside the realm of legal protection, we undercut the case against discrimination for everyone else.

Equal treatment under the law means that everyone belongs to the human community.

Abortion undermines the foundation of feminism and poisons the well against civil rights for African Americans, the elderly, the disabled, and others.

Marilyn Kopp
Cleveland

Kopp is a member of Feminists for Life.

The Plain Dealer
Tuesday, April 22, 2008

47

The Ol' Conception Question

I found your article "Bitter Pill," and the letters that followed, to be disturbing and misleading. They presented as undisputed fact the opinions that pregnancy begins when the fertilized egg implants in the uterus, not at fertilization, and that morning-after pills, which prevent implantation, are therefore not abortifacients but are contraceptives that prevent pregnancy.

These opinions have been widely refuted within the medical and scientific communities. At least 10 medical dictionaries define pregnancy as beginning at conception. Instead of engaging in semantic gymnastics, which deny that abortion and emergency contraception take human life, *Scene* should write about support available to women that enables them to take control of their lives without having to sacrifice their offspring. Organizations such as the Nurturing Network, for example, provide practical assistance with housing, college transfers, work assignments at sympathetic companies, "phone buddies" who've been in the same situation, psychologists to work through the separation process of adoption, and pre- and postnatal medical care, all free or at sliding-scale fees.

Marilyn Kopp
Feminists for Life
Cleveland

Scene
August 10–16, 2005

48

Pro-lifers: They're Not All Geeks Anymore

Thanks to Laura Putre for dispelling stereotypes of pro-lifers as geeky old right-wing misogynists ["Nouveau Womb"]. The Human Rights Youth Resistance reflects a growing trend among young people rejecting abortion and supporting life-affirming alternatives. They join with several nontraditional pro-life groups in consistently opposing violence against any individual, from womb to tomb. Thanks for the thoughtful profile.

Marilyn Kopp
Feminists for Life
Cleveland

Scene
September 4–10, 2002

49

Feminists for Life Respond

Thank you for your fascinating and chilling interview with "Anonymous Abortionist" (July 12). I understand why he wants to remain anonymous, since abortionists are so highly stigmatized, even by other doctors who claim to favor abortion availability. Still, I would have liked to know who he is so that I could exercise my "right to choose" another practitioner for my medical care.

A doctor who believes that it is "safer" to induce a breech birth and then pause it in the middle to kill the child is a doctor who is not paying attention to the American Medical Association, which says such a procedure is never medically indicated.

In fact, the abortionist was unable to cite one specific circumstance in which this procedure might be needed. One reason for this inability might have been that partial-birth abortion provides the best specimens for those who traffic in fetal body parts, and the most profits for the doctors who perform them. This lucrative business was recently exposed on *20/20* and has since prompted congressional hearings.

Many late-term abortions occur because the woman really doesn't want an abortion. Mistakenly believing late-term abortions are illegal, she hides the pregnancy until it's too late—she hopes—to be pressured. Partial-birth abortion doesn't protect a woman—it provides an escape hatch for the father, her family, and her employer or school, who should stand by her, but, through their lack of support, instead pressure her to have the abortion she had tried for months to avoid.

In claiming that a ban on this procedure places an "undue burden" on women, the Supreme Court justices have once again pitted women against their children. No matter how it is worded or how it is performed, abortion hurts women. This won't stop until women stand together and declare it unacceptable, that we deserve better. Lack of emotional and financial resources is the real undue burden—and abortion will never lift that.

Marilyn Kopp, Executive Director
Feminists for Life of Ohio
Cleveland

Cleveland Free Times
July 26–August 1, 2000

50

In the Aftermath of Roe vs. Wade: Pro-choice Advocates Forget a History of Oppression

Twenty-seven years ago, the US Supreme Court legalized abortion and ignited a controversy that grows more heated each year. The court's 1973 *Roe vs. Wade* ruling upheld a woman's right to privacy. But in doing so, has the court unintentionally desensitized us to the value of all human life?

Before *Roe vs. Wade*, abortion arguments centered on when life begins, but the court's ruling ducked this question and addressed only the issue of privacy. The court's refusal to acknowledge the personhood of the developing child, even though the child is both human and alive, is a familiar one. In the 1857 Dred Scott decision, for example, the court ruled that slaves were not fully human and were only the property of their owners. The avoidance is coming back to haunt us.

For 27 years, following the model of *Roe vs. Wade*, our public debate has ignored the issue of life and instead pits the woman's right to privacy against the rights of her in-utero child. This argument presumes that the woman and her child are adversaries and that the courts have to favor one at the expense of the other. When the court "chose" women, it effectively subsumed the human right to life under the lesser (though significant) right to privacy. Surely, elevating the right to privacy over the right to human life diminishes the value we put on life.

But in fact, the argument doesn't need to be framed this way—woman against fetus. We could revisit the underlying, now-neglected issue of when life begins. On this, the pro-life and pro-choice sides seemed to have moved closer together.

Since 1973, technological advances such as ultrasound and laparoscopy have given us unprecedented insights into fetal life. Genetic research has firmly established the humanity of the in-utero child, whose 6,000 unique characteristics in the earliest days of development are being mapped.

Now even prominent pro-choice scholars such as Catharine MacKinnon, Carol Gilligan, and Germaine Greer acknowledge that abortion takes a human life. They justify this, however, by saying that women, just like men, may at times have the right to make life-and-death decisions for others. This mentality reveals no new understanding of justice but a tragic repetition of the struggle for domination and power: The victims become the victimizers; the oppressed become oppressors.

It wasn't until 1920 that US women were acknowledged as fully human. Prior to that, feminists fought against their status as chattel—property of their husbands or fathers, whose worth was dependent on their desirability to a man. The feminists of the 19th century—most of them abolitionists as well—asserted the equality of all human beings, maintaining that men's greater strength or their traditional status did not justify the subjugation of women. In other cultures, baby girls are routinely murdered because they are less desirable than boys. Now, it seems, pro-choice women are adopting the traditional arguments of oppressive men. Life is valuable, in other words, when we decide it is.

In contrast, pro-life feminists like Daphne de Jong continue to advance the truly feminist argument that all human beings are equally valuable: "The feminist claim to equality is based on the equal rights of all human beings. The most fundamental of all is the right to life. If women are to justify taking this right from the unborn, they must concede that their superiority of size, of power or of physique or intellect or need, or their own value as a person transcends any right of the unborn. In the long history of male chauvinism, all these have been seen as good reasons for withholding human rights from women." And, it might be added, all these have been used to justify slavery, capital punishment, war, and other forms of violence by a patriarchal society.

As pro-life feminist Linda Naranjo-Huebl suggests, when a pro-choice woman states that she must control her own body, ask her to try to restate the problem. Within her range of thinking about the law and rights and autonomy, she recognizes no model, no paradigm, by which both the woman's and the child's rights can be respected simultaneously. What this says is not that pro-lifers should stop listening to her but, rather, urge her to move beyond the patriarchal thinking that recognizes only either/or situations. Women often "choose" abortion because they feel they have no other choice. By facilitating access to health care, making adoption more appealing, instilling healthy self-images toward our bodies, and supporting women and children instead of abandoning and scorning them, we multiply women's choices while truly upholding the value of all human lives.

Kopp is executive director of Feminists for Life of Ohio.

Marilyn Kopp
The Plain Dealer
Friday, January 21, 2000

Readers Speak Out on Preterm, Abortion: Abortion "Hurtful to Women"

In a less-than-objective article on Carolyn Buhl and Preterm abortion clinic, the *Plain Dealer* gave short shrift to the concerns of pro-lifers and no consideration whatsoever to our arguments.

First, positive terms were used for those defending abortion, while negatively charged terms were used for the pro-life side.

Also, the photos reinforced false media stereotypes of pro-lifers as religious and male. Yet when interviewed, Denise Mackura and I each made our case against abortion on a civil rights/feminist basis, not a religious one. And obviously, we're both female, as are the vast majority of pro-life organizers and activists.

Regarding Buhl's comments that "Everyone is doing the best they can under the circumstances, based on their own experiences. It is not my role to judge," it seems that certain feminists have no problem confronting other forms of abuse or violence, but when it comes to abortion, they suddenly hide behind euphemisms. Pro-lifers don't oppose "terminating pregnancies" at Preterm. Pregnancies are meant to be terminated; we just think it should happen at around nine months. Our objection is to killing children.

In characterizing the pro-life side, however, the article's language became harshly negative. The timeline of "milestones" in the abortion debate, for instance, characterized 1994 as "the bloodiest year ever for abortion clinic violence." While clinic shootings are reprehensible, the *Plain Dealer* hypocritically failed to take into account the violence *inside* clinics—35 million times since *Roe vs. Wade.*

The sad reality is that none of the people who wrote about their feelings in the journal at Preterm *wanted* an abortion. Out of despair, they felt they had no other choice. Yet alternatives and support existed … to keep their lives and bodies intact, as well as their children's.

In the 25 years since Preterm was founded, it's no coincidence that public support for abortion has diminished—particularly among women and young people.

We've seen an increase in life-affirming reproductive choices for women, including better medications to treat postpartum depression, to which Buhl attributed her decision to abort 30 years ago; more attractive adoption options; better child-support enforcement; more free pregnancy resource centers; and increased awareness of sexual harassment and violence against women. True progress lies in eliminating the problems that force women to choose between their life goals and their own children.

Marilyn Kopp
Executive Director
Feminists for Life of Ohio

The Plain Dealer
Tuesday, October 26, 1999

52

Praise for DeMarco

Thank you for your cover story by Laura "Brave Soul" DeMarco. Not only were Feminists for Life gagged at Lilith Fair, but so many words were put in our mouths in the letters that followed, I must clarify our stance:

FFL takes no position on birth control or contraception unless it acts as an abortifacient. We do not organize pickets at abortion clinics—it's not our style. FFL unequivocally condemns violence against abortionists or anyone. (We oppose abortion *because* we oppose violence.)

River Smith's claim that FFL was not censored at Lilith Fair because we could have distributed our literature is false. Had we done so, according to the Cuyahoga Falls Law Department, we would have risked arrest for trespassing (even though we'd purchased tickets) since Sarah McLachlan had control of the Blossom grounds for what she marketed as "a celebration of women and music."

Ironically, Smith pointed out that "unless people are taught the real history of [any liberation] movement, they don't realize the full nature of the struggle." Yet he displayed his own ignorance of history by characterizing abortion as one of feminism's "most basic notions."

To the contrary, the founders of the American feminist movement unanimously opposed abortion and scathingly condemned it as "child murder," "infanticide," and "feticide." They railed against solving a "problem" with violence, letting men off the hook, and picking on beings weaker than ourselves. They opposed abortion not because the procedure was less safe

73

at the time but because it took a human life and ultimately hindered justice for women.

The current and aberrant feminist defense of abortion is an example of how deeply the roots of sexism run in our culture. Instead of embracing abortion as a basic right, we need to eradicate its root causes—the oppression and sexual exploitation of women that enable abortions to flourish.

Marilyn Kopp
Feminists for Life of Ohio
Cleveland

Cleveland Free Times
October 13–19, 1999

Note: See Laura DeMarco's articles about Lilith Fair and FFL in Part 2 of this book.

53

More Women Are Taking the Pro-life Position

In his Aug. 22 column "Women will be key to 2000 election," Thomas Brazaitis stated that Republican presidential contender Elizabeth Dole, who is pro-life, will have a hard time competing with the Democratic Party for the "women's vote" on the abortion issue.

To the contrary, the Democratic position, and specifically Al Gore's advocacy of abortion on demand, is very much at odds with the views of a majority of American women.

According to former Planned Parenthood president Faye Wattleton's New York-based Center for Gender Equity, 53 percent of American women now oppose abortion and think it should be illegal except in cases of rape, incest, or to save the life of the mother. This represents an 8 percent shift toward the pro-life position within the last two years.

The shift is not surprising. Since the 1973 *Roe vs. Wade* decision, women have opposed abortion in greater numbers than have men. Perhaps women realize it's unfair to have to choose between giving up their life goals and dreams or sacrificing their own children, a choice that men are never forced to make.

Brazaitis's stereotyping of women on this vital issue is misleading and inaccurate.

Marilyn Dickstein Kopp
Cleveland

Kopp is executive director of Feminists for Life of Ohio.

The Plain Dealer
Tuesday, August 31, 1999

54

Free-Spirited Woodhull Didn't Advocate Abortion

In her March 23 column, Ellen Goodman compared Elizabeth Dole—the "First Serious Female Contender for the Presidency"—with Victoria Woodhull, the first-ever female contender, who in 1870 ran for president 50 years before women could vote.

While lamenting Dole's rigidity, Goodman quoted the bold, free-spirited Woodhull on several aspects of women's legal, sexual, and economic rights. Yet Goodman blatantly omitted Woodhull's choicest words on probably the most controversial aspect of women's equality today—abortion.

Rather than defending abortion, as Goodman has done in the past, Woodhull scathingly condemned it. Writing in 1875, Woodhull insightfully linked abortion to society's oppression of women: "Men must cease from insulting all of womanhood by saying that freedom means the degradation of woman. Every woman knows that if she were free, she would never bear an unwished-for child, nor think of murdering one before its birth." Woodhull opposed abortion not because the procedure was less safe at the time but because it took a human life and ultimately hindered justice for women.

Goodman yearned for the passionate Woodhull, who, according to a colleague, "gave women the idea that they could own themselves." Goodman lamented, "Where, oh where, are the Victorias when you need them?" One might instead ask, Where are the feminist columnists when you need them to

76

challenge the conventional wisdom that women must violently
dispose of their own children in order to be equal?

Marilyn Dickstein Kopp
Cleveland

The Plain Dealer
Thursday, April 15, 1999

55

To Life

Thank you for Lisa Chamberlain's illuminating interview with Carolyn Buhl of Preterm abortion clinic (One Public Square, March 3). Of particular interest was Buhl's insistence that abortion not be secretive, yet throughout the entire interview, not one word was mentioned of the procedure itself.

The ugly reality of abortion—the dismembered and clearly discernible body parts of a woman's own child, even in her first trimester—is what's made this issue arguably the most contentious of our century.

Buhl dismisses evidence—again, avoiding uncomfortable reality—that most American women now oppose abortion and think it should be illegal except for rape, incest, or life of the mother. Buhl attributes this rethinking of abortion attitudes to a hostile "climate" created by pro-lifers, a climate that, according to Buhl, also supports the death penalty.

Contrary to public perception, studies in *Psychology Today* have shown that pro-lifers are actually less likely to support the death penalty than pro-choicers are. Not surprising. Both capital punishment and abortion view certain life as dispensable if it's burdensome or inconvenient. Both seek to kill that which one can't control—the same mentality, by the way, that justifies the use of violence against abortionists.

As support for abortion dwindles, we've seen an increase in life-affirming reproductive choices for women, including better medications to treat postpartum depression; more attractive adoption options; better child support enforcement; more free pregnancy resource centers; and increased awareness of sexual harassment and violence against women. True progress for women lies in eliminating the problems that force women to choose between their life goals and their own children—a choice that, after all, men aren't forced to make.

As support for abortion diminishes, so should support for the death penalty. Opposition to both reflects a consistent rejection of violence as a solution to human problems.

Marilyn Dickstein Kopp
Feminists for Life of Ohio
Cleveland

Cleveland Free Times
March 17–23, 1999

56

Twenty-Six Years Later, Abortion Debate Still Raging: Pro-lifers Are Stereotyped, Demonized

This Friday marks the 26th anniversary of the *Roe vs. Wade* decision, yet the abortion controversy continues to rage. In 1973, the nine-member, all-male Supreme Court legalized a procedure that, while intended as a last resort, has now become practically a way of life—one out of four US pregnancies today ends on the abortion table.

While the media have cast the debate as liberals vs. conservatives and as those supporting women's rights vs. those supporting the rights of the fetus, perhaps some new questions are in order. Is defense of abortion a liberal concept? Can't one simultaneously support both women's and unborn children's rights, or are they mutually exclusive? Can women's rights exist independent of other human rights?

For the last quarter century, many pro-lifers have been frustrated by their media portrayal (and therefore in public perception) as religious and political conservatives. While the "far right" make up one element of the pro-life movement, it's hardly the only one. Consider the Seamless Garment Network (SGN), a strong but often ignored national coalition of diverse groups and individuals such as the Pro-Life Alliance of Gays and Lesbians, Feminists for Life, the Dalai Lama, environmentalist Wendell Berry, and civil libertarian Nat Hentoff. The SGN consistently seeks to protect all life threatened, as their mission statement points out, by "war, abortion, poverty, racism, domestic violence, the arms race, the death penalty and euthanasia."

Pro-lifers are often painted as intolerant religious fanatics. Yet the abortion mentality that decrees, "It's a baby if I want it, it's a fetus if I don't," reflects the ultimate intolerance. History has shown time and again that when we value any class of individuals (be they women, minorities, gays, lesbians, Jews, the unborn, the disabled) based on our emotional reaction to them, we are simply rationalizing prejudice.

Feminist support for abortion seems particularly ironic considering that we have long ago rejected the notions that women are the property of their husbands or that a woman's worth depends on her desirability to a man. Is it not the height of hypocrisy to turn around and impose the same unjust standards on our children?

Many feminists insist that abortion is necessary for women to participate freely and equally in society. Anyone who disagrees, they argue, has merely adopted patriarchal standards and accepted women's "place" in society. Yet this argument demonstrates how deeply the roots of sexism run in our culture. Its premise is a sexist one—that women are inferior to men and that in order to be equal, we have to change our biology to become like men, wombless and unpregnant at will. What other oppressed group in history has had to undergo surgery in order to be equal?

What man has had to choose between a career and fatherhood? Between personal fulfillment and his child? Why are we putting up with this oppressive nonchoice?

It's been said that if men got pregnant, abortion would be a sacrament. But as feminist historian Mary Krane Derr writes, "If we truly valued the people who got pregnant, pregnancy would be the sacrament." Then abortionists, she adds, would have to lay down their instruments and seek rightful employment.

Sound like an idealistic dream? Not really. There are more

pregnancy care centers in the US than abortion facilities. And while lunatic clinic shooters grab most headlines, few people are aware of the multitude of free abortion-alternative services that are available in their own backyards.

Recently, Feminists for Life introduced a nationwide College Outreach Program. (College-aged women have the most abortions, and the group most supportive of abortion rights is college-aged men.) This program is designed to educate students and advisors about available resources so that no woman feels compelled to choose between her child and her college career. Ironically, the program—which also lobbies for services such as housing for pregnant students, on-site day care, adoption counseling, and maternity coverage in student health care plans—was met by fierce opposition from many "pro-choice" groups.

Like the death penalty and military aggression, abortion reflects society's tendency to solve problems by violently disposing of those who present the problems. Giving voice to the voiceless—not exerting lethal control over them—has always been a priority of the left.

On this *Roe vs. Wade* anniversary, pro-lifers will undoubtedly continue to be stereotyped as intolerant, right-wing, misogynist homophobes. This stereotype might make people feel more comfortable, but it underestimates the diversity of the pro-life movement and the subtleties and depths of its arguments.

Labeling is much easier than thinking.

Kopp is past president of Feminists for Life of Ohio.

Marilyn Dickstein Kopp
The Plain Dealer
Friday, January 22, 1999

Please note this article also appeared in the following newspapers:

Abortion Wars Undiminished 22 Years after *Roe vs. Wade*: Pro-life Forces Besmirched
The Columbus Dispatch
Friday, January 22, 1999

Roe vs. Wade Anniversary Renews Abortion Debate
Guest Opinion: Marilyn Dickstein Kopp is the past president of Feminists for Life of Ohio.
The Cincinnati Enquirer
Friday January 22, 1999

Pro-life Advocates Include Liberals
Marilyn Dickstein Kopp
The Indianapolis News
Tuesday, January 19, 1999

Choice?

In her Nov. 4 letter, Deborah Van Kleef criticized Jeff Harwood for implying in his profile of Yuriko Kawaguchi that, as a convicted felon with a prior misdemeanor, Kawaguchi, a "bad girl," was "undeserving" of an abortion. As if "good girls" deserve abortions? Van Kleef has things mixed up.

It's a degrading experience to pay an abortionist so you can take off your clothes, lie flat on your back, spread your legs, and have him go up inside you with sharp instruments to dismember your own child. How can this possibly be seen as an "empowering" experience that women deserve rather than the personal tragedy that it is?

When told about the support that's available—from family (in the case of Kawaguchi when she confided in them) or from the community (several individuals and organizations came forward to offer Kawaguchi medical and financial help, adoption assistance, counseling, housing, etc.)—desperate women like Kawaguchi don't even have to consider making this abhorrent choice: my kid or my college career.

Outrage that she didn't have the "choice" to kill her kid (especially a near viable one) seems a sick perspective in our culture, one that drives a wedge between women and their own children. Not much of a feminist perspective of inclusivity, justice, or nonviolence, if you ask me.

Marilyn Dickstein Kopp
Feminists for Life of Ohio

Cleveland Free Times
November 11–17, 1998

58

First Feminists Were Opposed to Abortion

The US feminist movement was formally organized 150 years ago in Seneca Falls, NY. While the "Declaration of Women's Sentiments" drafted at that historic gathering set forth many demands, the movement became cohesive and powerful by focusing attention on a single goal—securing the right to vote.

Women's Equality Day today commemorates the achievement of that goal—after a 75-year battle—with the ratification of the 19th Amendment in 1920, granting political enfranchisement to women.

A second wave of the women's movement, ignited 30 years ago by Betty Friedan's landmark book *The Feminine Mystique*, once again galvanized support by rallying behind another legislative mandate—legalized abortion. As we assess the impact that these two legislative campaigns have had on our ongoing fight for equal rights, some important distinctions bear noting.

Most mainstream feminist groups today consider abortion the cornerstone of women's rights. Indeed, modern accounts of the suffrage campaign often draw parallels between anti-suffragists, who thought it "unladylike" for women to have a voice, and contemporary anti-abortion advocates, who want to deny women their reproductive freedom and keep them in their place—shackled to babies and the kitchen sink.

Because modern feminism seems to be synonymous with abortion rights, few people are aware that the founders of the American feminist movement were staunchly opposed to abortion and scathingly condemned it as a "most degrading and disgusting crime" (Elizabeth Cady Stanton), "ante-natal murder" (Sarah Norton), and the "ultimate exploitation of women" (Alice Paul).

Why would such progressive champions of women's equality unanimously oppose such a fundamental "right"? For the same reason that many of the suffragists also were abolitionists: They believed that every individual, regardless of race or gender, is entitled to basic human rights and dignity and that those rights could not be given or taken away by others. Stanton wrote in 1873, "When we consider that women are treated as property, it is degrading for women to treat their children as property, to be disposed of as they see fit." [See footnote on letter number 34.]

But the early feminists' pro-life views went well beyond the anti-abortion rhetoric of their day. They argued that in order to eliminate the "evil" of abortion, we must reach the root cause—society's oppression of women. Victoria Woodhull, free-love advocate and first woman presidential candidate, wrote in 1875, "Every woman knows that if she were free, she would never bear an unwished-for child, nor think of murdering one before its birth." The early feminists recognized abortion as a symptom of women's oppression, not a solution to it, and they looked forward to its elimination rather than its wholesale acceptance.

The drive for legal abortion in the late 1960s came in response to legitimate social problems that were preventing women from reaching their fullest potential: an unfair burden on women for nurturing children while men were given more opportunities for achievement outside the home, pay inequity, job discrimination, sexual harassment, domestic violence, and a lack of legal and financial rights.

The right to vote was considered by many to be the "red herring of the revolution" because it did not bring about the desired results. Most women ended up voting like their husbands and in low numbers at the polls (only recently surpassing men). And although some progress has been made in achieving equal representation, we still have a long way to go to reach parity.

But while suffrage didn't achieve all of the goals that its proponents expected, neither did it detract from them. Abortion, on the other hand, directly contradicts the feminist values that drove the movement's fight for equality. Emphasis on abortion has hindered progress in achieving real reforms that would advance our legitimate goals.

Rather than liberating women, abortion liberated men from obligations to their partners and children. Child abuse and the feminization of poverty have escalated since the availability of abortion, and instead of shared responsibility, more of the burden of child rearing has shifted to women. By giving in to abortion instead of working for social changes that would facilitate combining children and career, we have relieved society of its obligation to accommodate the real needs of women.

Women for abortion rights have abandoned core feminist values and have adopted the worst patriarchal standards: seeking power through control, condoning violence on the grounds of personal privacy, and using killing to resolve conflict. By insisting on abortion as a necessary component to equality, we have capitulated to a traditional worldview. In effect, women must become wombless and unpregnant like men to fit in, and they must resort to violence to do so.

As the feminist movement continues into the next century, women must re-evaluate the causes around which we rally in order to reach our goal of a more inclusive society. Rather than abortion, which has not brought us closer to our goal, let us support causes that reflect true feminist ideals of justice and nonviolence, causes that actually will bring women the respect they deserve. Then we can declare in full confidence, as Susan B. Anthony did in her last publicly spoken words, that "failure is impossible."

Kopp is president of Feminists for Life of Ohio.

Marilyn Dickstein Kopp
The Plain Dealer
Tuesday, August 26, 1997

Please note this article also appeared in the following newspaper:

True Feminist Stances Include Pro-life
Marilyn Dickstein Kopp
The Indianapolis News
Tuesday August 26, 1997

59

Life and Women Still Are Not Valued

In her July 8 *Everywoman* column, Eleanor Mallet examined the tragic case of Melissa Drexler, the 18-year-old who allegedly gave birth to, then killed, her infant at the high school prom. Columnist George Will linked Drexler's lack of respect for her newborn's life to the 1973 Supreme Court decision legalizing abortion. Mallet dismissed this link, stating the killing of newborns in the first 24 hours after birth has declined since the availability of abortion. But what happens after the first 24 hours? According to a 1991 *Plain Dealer* article, "Mothers biggest homicide peril to tots, study says," homicide is the fourth-leading cause of death among US children ages 1–4, representing a six-fold increase in the last 30 years. The most frequent perpetrator is the child's own mother. While increased violence has many causes, this statistic is particularly sobering, considering the court's anti-feminist ruling in 1973 that the unborn child is now the "property" of the mother and that the child's worth is dependent on how wanted or valued she or he is.

According to Mallet, the most common reason for killing newborns is that they are "unwanted." They are not "unwanted." The average wait on a list to adopt newborns in Ohio is three to five years. There are waiting lists of people wanting to adopt babies with Down syndrome (the National Down Syndrome Adoption Exchange) as well as babies who have spina bifida or who are HIV-positive.

It's true, as Mallet says, that "it was ... a tragedy that [Drexler] was so profoundly isolated that she confided in no one who might have helped her deal with her situation."

Our society has been so unresponsive to the needs of females that girls aren't raised to know how strong they can be and to be able to resist advances of "predatory" males, thus avoiding pregnancy in the first place. And the girls, once in the predicament of an unplanned pregnancy, are fearful of seeking help. The ready availability of abortion does little to alleviate the shame of the girl or to encourage life-affirming alternatives for both her and her child. Instead, the girl's "problem" is taken care of by violently disposing of the child out of sight in a sanitized clinic, rather than at a high school prom. In the words of the great pro-life feminist Susan B. Anthony, "When we consider that women are treated as property, it is degrading for women to treat their children as property, to be disposed of as they see fit." *

Perhaps Mallet would agree that the perceived "need" for abortion would not exist in a society that truly valued females and their reproductive capacities.

Please note the above quote was mistakenly attributed to Susan B. Anthony.

Marilyn Dickstein Kopp
Cleveland
Elizabeth Shoemaker
Avon

Kopp is president and Shoemaker is vice president of Feminists for Life of Ohio.

The Plain Dealer
Friday, July 25, 1997

60

Bravo Sowd!

Congratulations to David Sowd ("Reality Check," June 5–11) for showing how abortion conflicts with true feminist ideals of justice, nonviolence, and nondiscrimination.

While women with unplanned pregnancies face very real problems and pressures, we can work through those problems in life-affirming ways that don't involve killing.

To readers who find themselves in that situation, please know that you are not alone. For real solutions that can keep both your life and your child's intact, contact one of the pregnancy care centers listed under "Abortion Alternatives" in the Yellow Pages.

As Sowd's piece forces us to acknowledge, true justice for women must be built on a foundation of nonviolence. Women deserve better than the lousy "choice" of abortion.

Marilyn Dickstein Kopp
President, Feminists for Life of Ohio
Cleveland

Scene
June 12–18, 1997

61

Veto Can't End Debate on Partial-Birth Issue

The most dreaded "complication" of a late-term abortion is the production of a live baby. When confronted with the reality of their philosophical abstractions—a gasping, wriggling baby struggling to live—abortion advocates must concede that the abortion was a failure because the child did not die. The unexpected revival of the partial-birth abortion ban, thought to be killed by President Bill Clinton's veto last year, is an appropriate metaphor for their dilemma.

Congress once again is poised to send the president a bill that would ban this particularly gruesome abortion technique, in which the abortionist drags a well-developed baby feet first from her mother's uterus, then kills her by stabbing her in the skull and sucking out her brain. Abortion apologists are terrified that the horrific truth about this procedure will subvert their most sacred tenet: Abortion must be allowed at any time for any reason.

The partial-birth abortion technique evolved from the "D&E" procedure in which the baby is dismembered while still in the uterus and the body parts are removed one by one. This method was problematic because the abortionist was working blindly; the mother was at risk of being injured by his instruments and by her baby's broken bones. Nevertheless, for years the D&E was the preferred method for late abortions—supplanting the older technique of inducing premature labor—because D&E guaranteed a dead baby.

For this reason, the partial-birth procedure is fiercely defended by the abortion lobby, even though women actually may be harmed by it. This technique was invented and

92

promoted by a couple of ordinary abortionists; it has not been submitted to peer review or to controlled studies that would establish its safety.

Clinton defended his veto of the ban by stating that partial-birth abortions protect the future fertility of women, even though one of the women who stood behind him at the veto ceremony has had five miscarriages since her partial-birth abortion. (This is not surprising. The partial-birth technique requires that the cervix be mechanically forced open to make room for the removal of the rather large baby, which sometimes results in an "incompetent" cervix that cannot protect future pregnancies.)

Clinton also proclaimed that partial-birth abortions are performed only in cases in which the mother's life or health is at risk, or her baby is so malformed it has no chance of survival. Based on this belief, he has vowed to veto the bill again. Renowned pediatric surgeon and former surgeon general C. Everett Koop asserted in the *American Medical News* that the president was "misled by his medical advisors on what is fact and what is fiction."

Last August, the Physicians' Ad Hoc Coalition for Truth—a group of more than 400 distinguished professors and specialists in gynecology, obstetrics, and fetal medicine— declared that "Congress, the public—but most importantly, women—need to know that partial-birth abortion is never medically indicated to protect a mother's health or future fertility…. In no case is it medically necessary to partly deliver the child vaginally" and then kill her before completing delivery.

Most partial-birth abortions are, in fact, not done for medical reasons. One Ohio abortionist acknowledged in a 1993 interview with the *American Medical News* that 80 percent of the partial-birth abortions he does are "purely elective." Other abortionists have said they routinely perform the procedure for easily correctable fetal defects such as cleft palates or just because the mother is single, young, depressed, or poor. Clinton's disingenuous offer to sign a "compromise" bill that includes health exceptions for the mother would allow partial-birth abortions for all of these reasons, thereby preventing none.

The abortion lobby was spectacularly successful in suppressing the truth about partial-birth abortion until this year, when Ron Fitzsimmons, executive director of the National Coalition of Abortion Providers, admitted that he and others had lied about how many of these procedures are performed and why they are performed. He acknowledged that the "vast majority" of the thousands of partial-birth abortions every year are performed on "healthy fetuses and healthy mothers." Others admitted to lying when they claimed that the baby felt no pain during the procedure.

This is not the first time the pro-choice lobby has lied. Ever since the early days of the abortion debate, when advocates claimed that each year, 10,000 American women died as a result of illegal abortions (the true figure, according to the Centers for Disease Control, was 39 women dying from legal and illegal abortions combined in 1972, the year before the *Roe vs. Wade* decision), abortion apologists have misled legislators, the media, the public—and most despicably—women, about abortion.

Women should be outraged that horrific violence is promoted in the name of women's health and safety. The fact—now admitted by some abortion advocates—is that partial-birth abortion is never necessary to protect the mother's life or health. It was this big lie that made this horrendous procedure seem a necessary evil.

Now that we know better, we should share what we know

with Clinton and Ohio's Sen. John Glenn and urge them to support a ban on this unconscionable violence.

Kopp is president of Feminists for Life of Ohio.

Marilyn Dickstein Kopp
The Plain Dealer
Thursday, May 8, 1997

62

True Feminism, Motherhood Don't Clash

Are feminism and motherhood at odds? Eleanor Mallet posed the question to readers in her Everywoman column about Anne Roiphe's new book, "Fruitful: A Real Mother in the Modern World."

Authentic feminism and motherhood do not clash. They complement each other. The misperception that the two are at odds is largely due to establishment feminism's advocacy of abortion, for abortion is at odds with both feminism and motherhood.

If feminism is about justice as well as a woman's autonomy, then the means by which we achieve our goals must also be just. Equal rights for women cannot come at the expense of others, especially not at the expense of our preborn children.

If being equal means women have to resort to domination and violence to become wombless and unpregnant like men, then we have not achieved justice.

As Daphne de Jong writes, we "have simply adopted the standards of our oppressor and fashioned ourselves in his image."

By promoting abortion instead of working for social changes that would facilitate combining children and career, feminist leaders have betrayed the vast majority of working women who want to have children. If we truly valued women and their life-giving capacity, we would not force them to choose between their life goals and their offspring. Nor would we define such an abhorrent choice as "liberating."

In taking feminism to task for such inconsistencies and for its failure to address issues such as child care, we are not, to use

Mallet's term, "kicking feminism around." Confronting the movement's failures and being willing to work through them is, rather, a sign of deep commitment and love.

Marilyn Dickstein Kopp
Cleveland

Kopp is president of Feminists for Life of Ohio.

The Plain Dealer
Friday, January 10, 1997

63

Soapbox: Call It by Its Name

Congress is expected to vote this month on whether to override President Clinton's veto of the Partial Birth Abortion Act, a bill prohibiting a controversial late-term abortion procedure. Two months before the election, political considerations will undoubtedly cloud the debate. This is unfortunate, as the bill has far-reaching implications and deserves to be considered on its own merit.

The procedure in question, more akin to infanticide than abortion, involves pulling a living fetus feet first from the womb until all but the head is exposed. Surgical scissors are jammed into the base of the skull, a catheter is inserted, and the brain is suctioned out, causing skull collapse and death.

The bill President Clinton vetoed would ban this procedure. President Clinton defended his veto by insisting the procedure is sometimes necessary in cases of severe fetal deformities or to protect a woman's life (an exception covered by the bill) or health. Such claims have been uncritically reported as fact by mainstream media. The claims, however, directly conflict with the testimony of leading medical experts, women who've given birth to children with such conditions, and doctors who perform the procedure.

Renowned pediatric surgeon C. Everett Koop asserted in an August 19 interview in the *American Medical News* that the president was "misled by his medical advisors on what is fact and what is fiction" regarding the procedure. In a statement issued last month, the Physicians' Ad Hoc Coalition for Truth (PHACT)—a group of 320 distinguished professors and specialists in obstetric, gynecology, and fetal medicine—said that "Congress, the public—but most importantly—women need to know that partial-birth abortion is never medically indicated to protect a mother's health or future fertility." They explain that with certain abnormalities, such as hydrocephalus, the attending physician has to drain excess fluid from the brain to allow a vaginal delivery, and in some cases, a Cesarean section is indicated. "In no case is it medically necessary to partly deliver the child vaginally" and then kill the fetus before completing delivery.

PHACT noted that instead of protecting a woman, this procedure—which has never been evaluated in mainstream, peer-reviewed literature—can pose significant threats, possibly damaging her cervix or rendering her infertile.

Most partial-birth abortions are, in fact, not done for medical reasons. One Ohio doctor, one of the few who performs the procedure, acknowledged in a 1993 interview with the *American Medical News* that 80 percent of the partial-birth abortions he does are "purely elective." Other doctors admit they routinely perform the procedure for "minor or doubtful" fetal defects such as cleft palates or because the mothers are single, young, depressed, or poor.

Several women who gave birth to babies with conditions that President Clinton claimed would "rip" their bodies "to shreds" if they didn't have access to the procedure shared their stories with Congress. Health-care professional Jeannie French testified that a dying child doesn't need "help" dying, especially in such a violent and painful manner. The child needs compassionate care and comfort.

French should know. Her daughter Mary, who suffered from a condition that caused her brain to develop outside her skull, died peacefully in her father's arms six hours after birth. Her donated heart valves saved the lives of two Chicago infants.

Some activists reflexively defend the procedure because they fear banning it would lead to a repeal of legalized abortion. They are, as John Leo pointed out in *U.S. News & World Report*, "in the exact position of gun lobbyists who shoot down bans on assault weapons" for fear of further gun legislation. "They refuse," he continues, "on tactical grounds, to confront the moral issue involved."

Defending this procedure damages the credibility of the pro-choice movement, particularly those in the Democratic party, who profess support of the Americans with Disabilities Act in their platform, yet justify the killing of disabled babies in partial-birth abortion. The clear message sent to disabled people is that if they are less than perfect, then in the name of "compassion," they are better off dead.

Alison Davis, feminist writer and outspoken disability rights activist (who uses a wheelchair because of spina bifida), sums up the challenge this issue presents: "By supporting abortion ... as a 'right' ... on the grounds of handicap ... the [women's] movement denies us an identity as equal human beings worthy of respect.... True liberation for all will mean accepting a degree of responsibility for each other which maybe we escape now, but ... equality 'just for me' inevitably means oppression for someone else—which is unfair, inhumane, and ... ultimately unworkable."

Kopp is president of Feminists for Life of Ohio and serves on the National Steering Committee of the Common Ground Network for Life and Choice.

Marilyn Dickstein Kopp
Cleveland Free Times
Wednesday, September 25, 1996

64

Opening Dialogue for Women
Way "Beyond Beijing"

By refusing to allow a pro-life perspective to be presented at a workshop on abortion, organizers of the upcoming "Beyond Beijing" women's conference at Cleveland State University have adopted a style more akin to the Chinese government than inclusive sisterhood. *The Plain Dealer*'s coverage of the conference ("Women plan follow-up to Beijing parley," Everywoman, Aug. 27) was equally disturbing. Pro-choice women had the opportunity to state their case, while the specific arguments of pro-life feminists were not even mentioned. "You get used to what you're in, and you're brainwashed to think this is cool," conference chairwoman Dorothy Lemmey was quoted as saying, and I have to agree, given society's widespread acceptance of abortion. Women are sadly mistaken if they believe they've achieved equality, particularly if "choice" is one of the barometers.

The issue, we believe, is not "who chooses," but rather "what is being chosen." By insisting on abortion rights, pro-choice feminists have abandoned core feminist values and adopted the worst patriarchal standards—seeking power through control and using killing as a solution to conflict. By insisting that abortion is a necessary component to women's equality, we concede that women are inferior to men because, in order to be equal, we must change our bodies to be wombless and unpregnant at will—that is, to be like men. By allowing the National Abortion and Reproductive Rights Action League to present the information segment of the workshop, organizers have disregarded the concerns of prominent pro-choice scholars.

Yale law professor Catharine McKinnon, for example, argued that the "right to privacy" abortion argument legitimizes date rape and spousal abuse. Elizabeth Fox-Genovese noted that making individual autonomy ("choice") supreme contradicts a feminist commitment to nurturing and interdependency. Yes, let's have a dialogue! But if conference organizers truly want to enhance women's awareness of issues, they should open the dialogue by presenting a stimulating challenge, not by censoring views that don't mesh with their own. Only then can we begin to move toward some real resolutions.

Marilyn Dickstein Kopp
Cleveland

Kopp is president of Feminists for Life of Ohio and serves on the National Steering Committee of the Common Ground Network for Life and Choice, Washington, D.C.

The Plain Dealer
Friday, September 20, 1996

65

Teen Pregnancy and Early Sex: High Risk and High Stakes

Teen sex involves not only the potential of pregnancy but many serious health risks. There are more than 12 million episodes of sexually transmitted diseases (STDs) annually in the United States. Two-thirds of those cases afflict those under 25. These diseases can result in the destruction of both male and female reproductive systems. Even more serious, of course, is the threat of AIDS. The idea that condoms provide "safe sex" (i.e., protection from infection with the AIDS virus) is highly misleading. Studies show that condoms have a much higher failure rate for blocking AIDS viruses than they do for contraception. Viruses are much smaller than sperm, and fertility cycles mean that pregnancy is not always a possibility when there is sexual intercourse. For disease transmission, every sexual episode creates the possibility for infection. To promote condoms as providing "saf*er*" sex means accepting that a significant number of teenagers will become infected with diseases including AIDS, as well as become pregnant (since contraceptive use among teens is so unreliable). That is unacceptable. With the stakes so high, we should be aiming for risk elimination, not risk reduction.

Choice-oriented sex education does not adequately account for the psychological and emotional differences between children/teens and adults. Real harm may be caused by too-early information about sex that disturbs the latency period in children that is a normal part of development. Further, teens are not adults in their decision-making capacity. Because of their level of cognitive thinking, they need *directive* messages, not just presentation of options. Nondirective messages that discuss abstinence among a range of options have been shown to be not effective. Teens are notorious nonusers of contraceptives despite major efforts at education.

Contraception and condom use are a technological remedy to a problem that is not technological but social. What is needed are *norms* about teen sexual behavior that make early sexual intercourse the deviant behavior instead of early sex as the norm and abstinence as deviant. There is a basic need to define society's expectations for male/female relationships, generally, and for young people, specifically. Our message must be that effective teen pregnancy prevention requires respect for young women and relationships based on caring, equality, and commitment. This requires a comprehensive approach that goes far beyond sex education and programs to dispense condoms. Studies show that teenage girls don't want more sex education. They want help and support in saying "no."

In March of 1994 a group of students in Cleveland, Ohio, called "Young Adults with Voices" surveyed sixth through twelfth graders at 21 Cleveland public schools. Based on the survey results, the group presented a Youth Platform to local politicians that included the following proposals and recommendations: form support groups in schools for teens who want to choose sexual abstinence; hold regularly scheduled discussions promoting abstinence; encourage teens to abstain from sex until marriage.

There are communities that have dramatically reduced teen pregnancies by implementing cost-effective programs that guide teens toward abstinence by helping them assess who they are, where they want to go, and what will get them there. These programs have been extremely successful in preventing teen pregnancies, even in socio-economically depressed areas, by providing realistic alternatives, hope for a future, an ongoing presence of role models and mentors, activities including visits to colleges and cultural events, and assistance in securing scholarships. Many areas have recognized the need to ensure that these types of programs are available for boys as well as girls.

With the privilege of equality and freedom comes responsibility for sexual behavior. This idea must be instilled in both young men and young women. We must not shirk our obligation to provide young people with support and hope, nor underestimate their ability to respond. With our collective future at stake, we have the opportunity to make a difference. Let us not let our young people down.

Marilyn Kopp
The Network Papers
Search for Common Ground, 1996

Note: Contraception and sex education are outside of Feminists for Life's mission.

66

Health Protection That Hurts

President Bill Clinton recently vetoed a bill that would have banned partial-birth, late-term abortions, even though a February poll by Fairbank, Maslin, Maullin, and Associates showed that 78 percent of women voters supported the ban. In an election year when Clinton is courting the women's vote ("Clinton sees women tilting '96 election," April 13), women would do well to read between the "lines" offered by the president.

While acknowledging that the bill contained measures to protect the life of the mother, Clinton attempted to rationalize his actions by claiming that "health exceptions" were lacking. Such "health exceptions" are recognized by advocates on both sides of the debate as a tool to effectively kill proposed abortion legislation. In a typical male-dominated view of women's health, any bizarre reason is allowed as an exception, rendering the guidelines virtually meaningless.

As women physicians pointed out in congressional hearings, if a woman's health were truly at stake, we would not force labor for two to three days, deliberately induce a breech position, which is far riskier than normal delivery, and then abruptly halt the process seconds before the head emerges. If the living baby's torso, arms and legs can be safely delivered without endangering the mother's health, then the baby can just as easily be taken without having to jam scissors into her skull and suction her brains out.

As Dr. Warren Hern, author of the most widely used textbook on the procedure, said, "I would dispute any statement that this is the safest procedure to use."

Clearly, the purpose of Clinton's veto is not to protect women's health, as he maintains, but to defend the abortion, which in this case is virtually indistinguishable from infanticide. Women should be disgusted that this sickening violence is being perpetrated in our name and demand that Congress override this veto.

That women feel compelled to even make this kind of decision is a resounding indictment of how our society treats women and how it treats children. A truly compassionate society would not pit women's rights against the rights of their own children; what damages one will inevitably damage the other.

Marilyn Dickstein Kopp
Cleveland

The Plain Dealer
Tuesday, May 7, 1996

67

On Feminists for Life

I would like to thank Janet O'Donnell for her recent *Universe Bulletin* article about my work with Feminists for Life and to clarify some points in her thoughtful and well-written piece ("The Freedom to Choose Life," Feb. 9).

While Betty Friedan's landmark book of 1963, "The Feminine Mystique," helped form my early feminist consciousness, the book did not mention or promote abortion rights, as the article suggested. The current and aberrant feminist defense of abortion began later in 1966 when two men, Larry Lader and Dr. Bernard Nathanson of the National Association to Repeal Abortion Laws, convinced a reluctant Betty Friedan to include abortion as a civil right on the agenda of the National Organization for Women.

Soon after, abortion quickly and tragically grew to become the very symbol of women's equality. Dr. Nathanson, a former abortionist who has since accepted personal responsibility for the deaths of 60,000 preborn children, had a profound change of heart and is now an outspoken leader in the pro-life movement.

While some members of Feminists for Life had at one time been pro-choice, they joined our nonsectarian organization after gradually realizing that abortion was inconsistent, both historically and logically, with authentic feminist principles of justice, nonviolence, and nondiscrimination.

They further realized, as did our feminist foremothers, that support for women's rights and those of unborn children are not mutually exclusive. To the contrary, because we support

109

all human rights, we don't believe that women's rights can be won by sacrificing our offspring.

I have been gratified to see this pro-woman, pro-life message warmly embraced by many high school and college women within the secular community. They are coming to realize that the rights and dignity of all individuals, regardless of race, gender, economic status, stage of development, or place of residence, must be cherished, respected, and protected.

Marilyn Dickstein Kopp, president
Feminists for Life of Ohio
Cleveland

Catholic Universe Bulletin
February 23, 1996

68

Wrong People Are Called Intolerant

I found Eleanor Mallet's column (Jan. 23) about Tanya Melich's book, "The Republican War Against Women: An Insider's Report from Behind the Lines," disturbing and contradictory.

Melich, a lifelong Republican and, according to the book jacket, "a leader on the front lines of the pro-choice movement," accused the leadership of her party of "deliberately embracing a political strategy hostile to women." Melich complained about an "increasing intolerance for difference" among Republicans, yet displayed her own brand of intolerance by repeatedly and presumptuously characterizing opposition to abortion as "misogynist" and "anti-feminist."

In her bestselling book "Fire with Fire," influential feminist-author Naomi Wolf, a pro-choice liberal, warned against the use of such strict and damaging litmus tests to define feminism, declaring them misrepresentative of the views of the majority of women and an insult to their intelligence. Wolf found this to be particularly true with the contentious issue of abortion.

Granted, screaming "baby killer" and "murderer" makes it difficult to engage in constructive dialogue. But so do tendencies by the pro-choice movement to cloak abortion in evasive rhetoric and to refuse to acknowledge it as a moral inequity. Melich would do well to consider how such strategies have damaged feminist credibility and helped to create the backlash against women that she accused Republicans of exploiting. In a recent article in the New Republic, Wolf castigated pro-choice feminists for engaging in this callous and selfish devaluation of fetal life: "With the pro-choice rhetoric we use now, we incur three destructive consequences: hardness of heart, lying, and political failure."

The "intolerance for difference" that Melich lamented (and engaged in) is hardly unique to the Republican Party. Pro-life Democratic women have also experienced censorship of their views and a sense of abandonment by the party they felt always upheld the rights and dignity of the most vulnerable members of the human family.

If Melich is truly concerned about ending the war against women, I suggest she refrain from alienating millions of her pro-life sisters, acknowledge abortion for what it is—an injustice against fetal life that originates with injustice against female life—and work with us to help eradicate it.

Marilyn Dickstein Kopp
Cleveland

Kopp is president of Feminists for Life of Ohio.

The Plain Dealer
Monday, February 19, 1996

69

Misleading on ECPs?

I found your article "Emergency Pills After the Fact" (Oct. 25) disturbing and misleading. The article presented as undisputed fact the opinions that pregnancy begins when the fertilized egg implants in the uterus, not at fertilization, and that emergency contraceptive pills (ECPs)—which prevent implantation—are therefore not abortifacients but are contraceptives that prevent pregnancy.

These opinions have been widely refuted within the medical and scientific communities. At least ten medical dictionaries, including Mosby's, Dorland's, and Stedman's, in fact define pregnancy as beginning at conception and conception as beginning at fertilization, not implantation. This definition can also be confirmed by a number of embryology, obstetric, human anatomy, and physiology textbooks.

I found particularly ironic the comments by Phyllis Clay of Preterm that the media does not write about the things that "help you take control of your life." Given the biological definition of when pregnancy begins, it's obvious that chemical and surgical abortions, as well as ECPs, more accurately involve taking control of someone else's life.

Instead of engaging in semantic gymnastics that deny that abortion and ECPs take human life, the *Free Times* should write about support available to women that enables them to take control of their lives without having to sacrifice their offspring. Organizations such as the Nurturing Network, for example, provide practical assistance with housing, college transfers, work assignments at sympathetic companies, "phone buddies" who've been in the same situation, psychologists to work through the separation process of adoption, if chosen, and competent pre- and postnatal medical care, all free or at sliding-scale fees.

Writing about these resources is not a negative judgment on women who've chosen abortion. Rather, it can save many women from the pain of a decision they may make because they feel they have no other choice.

Marilyn Dickstein Kopp, president
Feminists for Life of Ohio

The Cleveland Free Times
Wednesday, November 8, 1995

70

Abortion Play Not "Balanced"

I recently attended a Beck Center performance of "Keely and Du," recipient of 1994's Best Play Award from the American Theater Critics' Association. The local production was made possible through the support of Planned Parenthood and other organizations and individuals.

While the drama was well acted, I found absurd the claims that pro-life and pro-choice arguments were logically and equally offered ("Beck presents both sides in abortion play," Sept. 30).

The pro-life perspective was presented by the most insulting and extreme stereotypes imaginable: religious fanatics who kidnap a pregnant victim of spousal rape, chain her to a bed in a basement, offer condescending judgments, force her to look at pictures of bloody fetuses, and attempt a coerced reconciliation with her abusive, alcoholic husband.

Imagine had the pro-choice view been advanced from the following real life scenarios: abortionists who mutilate or sexually molest patients while they're under anesthesia, counselors who lie to clients that their babies are unadoptable or mislead them about stages of fetal development (causing clients to later suffer lifelong trauma after viewing ultrasounds of subsequent children), or an abortion defender who shoots at a pro-life demonstrator and is jailed for attempted murder when he misses and the gun jams.

While such characterizations would have been obviously unfair and misrepresentative of the pro-choice movement, they certainly would have brought to this critically acclaimed play an element of balance that was lacking.

115

Marilyn Dickstein Kopp
Cleveland

Kopp is president of Feminists for Life of Ohio.

The Plain Dealer
Monday, November 6, 1995

71

"Choice" That Is No Choice

In her Aug. 31 letter *"Roe* affirms our choices," Preterm's Carolyn Buhl stated that "Being free and having choices for our lives is the essence of what it means to be an American." Buhl fails to acknowledge, however, that with freedom comes accountability for the consequences of our choices when they affect other individuals.

It was, in fact, the shock of seeing these other individuals—a freezer full of dead fetuses—that changed the mind of real-life "Jane Roe," Norma McCorvey, about abortion.

How can Buhl refer to an act of such despair as a "choice"? Women can choose to give up their life goals and dreams, or they can submit to an invasive, humiliating procedure that destroys their child. How fortunate, we have a choice!

Instead of adapting our bodies to be like a man's, unencumbered by pregnancy, we should be demanding that society change to accept and accommodate women. Not every woman need be a mother. But to regard woman's unique and powerful life-giving capacity as a disease or a deviation is to internalize attitudes of low self-esteem toward our own bodies.

Although much progress has been made in the fight for equal rights, the current and aberrant feminist defense of abortion is evidence of how deeply ingrained the roots of sexism are in our culture. Instead of embracing abortion as an integral right, feminists should be working to eradicate it by reaching the root causes—the oppression and sexual exploitation of women—that enable abortions to flourish.

Marilyn Dickstein Kopp
Cleveland

Kopp is president of Feminists for Life of Ohio.

The Plain Dealer
Friday, September 15, 1995

72

Readers Offer Opinions on the Conference on Women

Using abortion as a solution to women's empowerment misses the point. As our sisters in developing countries recognize, there are strong linkages between fertility rates and other factors such as level of education, income, and child survival rates. A more holistic approach emphasizing empowerment of women in these areas need not include abortion.

As Prime Minister Benazir Bhutto of Pakistan challenged participants at the Cairo conference, "I dream ... of a world where we can commit our social resources to the development of life and not to its destruction." She also warned the conference must not be viewed as "a universal social charter seeking to impose adultery, abortion ... and other such matters" on the rest of the world.

Pope John Paul II's recent apology to women was welcome; his views on abortion are more consistent with this holistic approach of empowerment for women.

Marilyn Dickstein Kopp, Cleveland

The Plain Dealer
Tuesday, August 1, 1995

73

Security for All

The decision by the leadership of the National Organization for Women to include a defense of abortion on the agenda for the recent March for Women's Lives was disappointing. In doing so, march organizers not only sacrificed credibility in their case against violence, but they also alienated millions of women who might otherwise have supported the event ("Groups rally against violence on women," April 10).

With its unrewarding advocacy of abortion on demand, NOW repeatedly has disregarded the legitimate concerns of many feminists who recognize abortion as a violation of authentic justice. Violence of any type is an abhorrent and unacceptable response to any social issue, as in the case of the despicable murders of abortionist John Britton and clinic escort James Barrett.

Contrary to the assertions of Feminist Majority Foundation leader Eleanor Smeal, the purpose of opposing abortion is not to control women. Smeal's argument would have more validity if pregnancy and childbearing were simple matters of women's autonomy. They are not, however; abortion involves direct lethal control over a genetically separate individual.

In fact, the demand for the right to confer personhood on the fetus only if she is wanted or valued by the mother is more reflective of a patriarchal understanding of equality and inclusion.

If we are to establish true justice, women's rights must be built on a foundation of nonviolence and must include respect for other human rights as well.

As Jesse Jackson stated at the March for Women's Lives,

"None of us are secure until all of us are secure." Unless we can extend security to the most vulnerable and defenseless members of the human family—while protecting individual rights of born members as well—there is no reason to believe any of us will be secure.

Marilyn Dickstein-Kopp
Cleveland

Dickstein-Kopp is president of Feminists for Life of Ohio.

The Plain Dealer
Wednesday, May 3, 1995

74

"Abortion Rights" Is a Strange
Way to Spell "Equality"

In his letter to the editor "Bad analogies, bad arguments on abortion issue" (May 26), David Goodman of Planned Parenthood contends that Louis Pumphrey's criticism of women with unintended pregnancies (letters, May 17) is borne of "intolerance and misogyny." The frustration articulated by Pumphrey reflects not an intolerance of women but rather an intolerance of injustice. Goodman fails to acknowledge that the greatest example of misogyny in our culture is manifest in abortion.

Women are the only group in history who have had to sacrifice their offspring for the "privilege" of participating freely and equally in society. Abortion perpetuates society's sexist double standard that forces women to choose between family and career, between children and personal fulfillment, but doesn't force men to make the same choices.

By capitulating to abortion, we have relieved society from its obligations to accommodate the real needs of women: safe and effective birth control, accessible pre- and postnatal care, affordable day care, and flexible work and school situations. These needs will never be adequately addressed as long as women are climbing up on the abortion table 1.6 million times a year to ensure the status quo.

This is not to say that women should be punished for having sex. Children are not punishment and should not be viewed as such. Having someone go up inside you with sharp instruments to dismember your child can be more reasonably viewed as punishment.

Goodman seems to blur the distinction between punishment and accountability. Along with the privilege of equality comes the responsibility of sexual behavior, and abortion does little to instill that responsibility in men or in women. It is not "intolerant" to expect women to be responsible for the consequences of their actions when they affect others. How are women to gain equality—the opportunity to serve as judges and senators, doctors and lawyers—without an assumption that women are quite capable of being accountable for their actions?

Abortion itself is inconsistent with authentic feminist principles of justice, nonviolence, and nondiscrimination. We have long rejected the notions of women being regarded as property of their husbands or that a woman's value is contingent on being wanted by a man. It is hypocritical to turn around and impose the same unjust standards on our children.

If the feminist movement is to maintain any credibility, we must be consistent in our demand for human rights. Abortion is, as Alice Paul (author of the original Equal Rights Amendment) put it, "the ultimate exploitation of women." If we truly espoused equality for women, we would refuse to choose abortion; we would refuse to choose to participate in our own oppression and that of our children.

Marilyn D. Kopp
Cleveland

Kopp is serving as president of Feminists for Life of Ohio.

The Plain Dealer
Monday, June 20, 1994

75

Abortion Pill Horrors Are Deeper than the "Political Climate"

Michael Unger's Aug. 8 article, "Political climate freezing out abortion pill," presents a limited perspective on the controversy surrounding RU-486. Unger blames anti-abortion activists for depriving US women access to the pill but fails to mention that even pro-choice activists have adamantly opposed RU-486.

Professor Janis G. Raymond, Renate Klein, and Lynette J. Dumble, in their "RU-486: Myths, Misconceptions and Morals" report, found the drug so dangerous they urged it be pulled from the market immediately. Particularly significant were researchers' findings that the complications, such as excessive bleeding and pain, were "often evaluated differently by researchers than by women themselves." The three authors argued that there was an unarticulated message that female pain was expected—in fact, that "pain that would be unnatural/intolerable for men is natural/tolerable for women." They concluded that "the medical [community's] acceptance, without comment or criticism, of what have now become 'minimal,' 'tolerable,' and 'acceptable' side effects for women deserves to be highlighted for what it is—unethical medical practice."

Aside from the physical risks, women face the emotional implications of enduring an anxious week at home, anticipating the expulsion of a dead fetus. This is not a price men are forced to pay for sex. Ironically, this traumatic experience was characterized by Edouard Sakiz, president of the French company that manufactures the drug, as "an appalling psychological ordeal."

However, the RU-486 controversy is not merely an argument of whether chemical or surgical intrusion does more harm to a woman's body. The introduction of RU-486 inescapably leads to questions of much deeper ramifications: Is our society willing to accept the concept of human life as disposable? Are we sold on the myth that women can achieve equality only by sacrificing their own children?

As Susan B. Anthony and the other founders of the feminist movement recognized, abortion is not a solution to inequality but a symptom of it. The introduction of RU-486 is yet the latest assault against women in an age-old battle. As Rachel McNair, president of Feminists for Life of America, has pointed out, "Some women insist abortion was the right decision but say it was painful and humiliating. This won't change with drugs, but only when it's not acceptable for women to feel it necessary to do something painful and humiliating."

Marilyn D. Kopp
Cleveland

Kopp is Cleveland-area director of communications for Feminists for Life of Ohio.

The Plain Dealer
Wednesday, September 8, 1993

76

Uncommon Cause, Common Ground

On January 14 of this year, FFL-Cleveland sponsored an intriguing discussion called *"Common Ground* in the Abortion Debate."* We were privileged to host four national speakers for the event: Andrew F. Puzder, B. J. Isaacson-Jones, and Jean Cavander, all members of the St. Louis Common Ground Association, and Jeannie Wallace French, founder of the National Women's Coalition for Life.

Common Ground is a unique concept in that it leaves unquestioned the basic dispute of "life versus choice." Rather it attempts to identify areas of mutual concern and seeks ways for advocates on both sides of the debate to work together in addressing these concerns.

Our initiative was inspired by an article in the Cleveland *Plain Dealer* that appeared a year previously about efforts pioneered in St. Louis by Puzzler and Isaacson-Jones. Former Clevelander Puzder had drafted the legislation for 1989's landmark *Webster v. Reproductive Health Services (RHS)* case. As director of RHS, the largest abortion provider in Missouri, Isaacson-Jones had sued to stop the legislation.

Six months after the Supreme Court upheld the Missouri law, Puzder wrote a commentary that suggested that it was time for both camps to put aside their hostilities and cooperate in helping the women and children whose interests they both claimed to protect. Isaacson-Jones took Puzder up on the offer and called, and a series of cordial discussions followed.

The two sides continue to advocate their positions on abortion but do not debate it with each other. They work together, instead, on issues of mutual concern: preventing unwanted pregnancies, teaching abstinence to teenagers, reducing infant mortality, assisting crack-addicted pregnant mothers, and financing school breakfast programs. The success of the dialogue initiated by legal adversaries Puzder and Isaacson-Jones has inspired a small "Common Ground" movement that has caught on in other cities, including Buffalo, Boston, and San Francisco.

FFL-Cleveland invited Puzder to speak at a public forum to initiate our Common Ground efforts, and Isaacson-Jones joined him. To round out the program, we invited Jeannie Wallace French.

We had apprehensions. Would we be misrepresented by the news media as "compromising" on the issue? Would we be shunned by our local pro-life community for collaborating with the "enemy"? However, not being ones to shy away from controversy, we proceeded. The results were inspirational. More than forty people from diverse backgrounds showed up on a stormy winter night. Isaacson-Jones explained that she had "never lost sight of the idea that the other side is not the enemy. We are political adversaries, not enemies. The enemy is unwanted pregnancies, poverty, ignorance, and racism. These enemies are common to us all."

Puzder stated that Common Ground is not a compromise and that both he and Isaacson-Jones continue to strongly support their respective positions on abortion. However, there are areas where they can agree without abandoning their principles. For example, he noted that aid to women and children in financially adverse situations should be clear common ground. Obviously, pro-lifers should support giving aid to these women and children, not only to prevent abortions but because we recognize that being pro-life is not something which ends at birth.

Pro-choicers should also support aid for these women and

children since a woman who makes the decision to abort for financial reasons is not really making a choice. She is being economically compelled to do something she would otherwise choose not to. After all, Puzder noted, one of the choices should be birth.

This sensible approach of working together to accomplish mutual goals evoked thorough, balanced, and supportive coverage from the news media. The pro-life position was fairly presented, and much to our surprise, no one accused anyone of compromise. No one who attended the discussion could have made such an accusation honestly.

The presentation generated overwhelming enthusiasm for establishing a Cleveland Common Ground group. We have adopted a modified version of the ground rules laid out in St. Louis:

- Do not debate abortion.
- Commit to a win/win problem-solving model.
- Do not use Common Ground to promote respective causes.
- Acknowledge that Common Ground members will, outside of the group, continue to promote and further their respective causes.
- Do not debate religion.
- Keep partisan politics out.

While our efforts are still new, we have been able to bring together a very dedicated group of individuals who are committed to a wide range of social issues. At our first follow-up meeting, we identified many worthwhile common ground activities, such as providing support to networks of assistance for pregnant women (i.e., the Nurturing Network); facilitating adoption alternatives; expanding access to prenatal and postnatal care; preventing domestic violence and abuse; eliminating legal/societal pregnancy discrimination; fostering gender awareness and equality; and promoting adolescent decision-making skills and positive self-image (male and female).

Although, as Isaacson-Jones stated, there are sometimes "more questions than answers," for now Common Ground has been a most gratifying experience: one not meant to replace debate but to complement it. The goodwill and sincerity of the people involved has been inspiring.

Yet Common Ground is not for everyone. It is a personality-intensive exercise that can be frustrating, risky, even painful. But as pro-life lawyer Karin V. Morin noted, "Working together will ultimately require talking to each other. My experience with the Public Conversations Project in Boston has given me some hope that dialogue is possible. I know it is essential in resolving the problem of abortion in our society." She adds, "I remain convinced that abortion is truly evil, an unacceptable solution to crisis pregnancy; yet I am equally convinced that only within a non-confrontational dialogue can we achieve, gradually, a societal consensus to that effect."

We all have good friends, colleagues, or even family members with whom we disagree on this issue. For those of us who are dismayed at the hostile divisiveness it has generated, Common Ground is a welcome approach.

In reflecting on Common Ground, I am often reminded of the beatitude, "Blessed are the peacemakers." As Frederica Mathewes-Green has pointed out, we are not often given the opportunity in our lifetimes to be peacemakers. By bringing harmony into a notoriously conflict-filled area, we can be empowered to solve problems that are common to us all.

Marilyn D. Kopp currently serves as Cleveland area director of communications for FFL of Ohio.

Marilyn Kopp
Sisterlife
(a publication of Feminists for Life of America)
Summer 1993

77

Real "Choice" Means Hearing
from Pro-life Groups, Too

Regarding John Corlett's March 30 letter to the editor, "Pro-life no-show at state hearings": We have a suggestion for Corlett the next time a worthy opportunity like testifying for Child and Family Health Services comes up. Instead of a postevent letter publicly condemning us for not attending, a simple phone call notifying us of the event in advance would be much more helpful!

Although Planned Parenthood can afford several full-time salaried employees like Corlett, our organization operates on a volunteer basis. Our members' first priorities must be career and family commitments. While Corlett was busy lobbying organizations across the state for testimony, why didn't he contact us? We would have loved to come!

As Corlett knows, Feminists for Life has long advocated this crucial support for women as essential in enabling them to make life-affirming choices. We have also attempted to encourage an atmosphere of cooperation and communication between pro-life and pro-choice organizations so that energy and resources spent fighting each other can be directed toward more constructive goals.

We hope Corlett takes advantage of our ongoing invitation to dialogue and includes us in future worthwhile endeavors, which in the long run benefit us all.

Marilyn D. Kopp
Cleveland

The Plain Dealer
Thursday, April 22, 1993

78

Real Freedom

Twenty years after *Roe vs. Wade*, women continue to subject themselves to invasive surgical procedures in their quest for equality. Sara Cort's Jan. 22 letter to the editor echoes the sentiment that abortion is "extremely important for women who want and need to be treated on an equal level with men in America."

In accepting medical technology as a solution to equality, we are accepting the sexist premise that nature made women inferior to men. The premise is, of course, false, and it is an insult to say women must change their biology to fit into society.

Cort claims that "the pro-life movement is only a mask for right-wing, anti-woman politics." Perhaps she also regards Susan B. Anthony, Elizabeth Cady Stanton, and the other founders of the feminist movement as "anti-woman," because they were unanimously opposed to abortion. These progressive women leaders were themselves quite liberated from the sexually repressive attitudes of their Victorian era. They opposed abortion not primarily because of its safety or lack thereof but because of its violent and exploitative nature.

Abortion symbolizes not freedom of choice but freedom to capitulate to male domination. As Victoria Woodhull, free-love advocate and the first woman to run for president, wrote in 1875, "Men must no longer insult all womanhood by saying that freedom means the degradation of woman. Every woman knows that if she were free she would never bear an unwished-for child, nor think of murdering one before its birth."

And women will never shed their second-class status if they continue to view themselves as requiring surgery to avoid it.

Marilyn D. Kopp
Cleveland

Kopp is Cleveland-area director of communications for Feminists for Life of Ohio.

The Plain Dealer
Monday, February 1, 1993

79

Signs of Bias?

The *Plain Dealer* attacked the Bush/Quayle campaign for disallowing signs at the president's Oct. 28 rally yet failed to mention that the Bill Clinton campaign maintains the exact same policy.

While we fully support the freedom of speech of AIDS activists Paul Schwitzgebel and James DeLong, we believe precautions should be taken if it appears that the safety of either the crowd or the protestors is endangered.

It's ironic that no mention was made of the abortion protestors at Hillary Clinton's appearance that same day. They were also shoved and pushed and had obscenities hurled at them and their signs knocked down. Perhaps if they had disingenuously arranged a front-row escort, unfurled hidden banners, and shouted down Mrs. Clinton, they too would have received coverage. But it's doubtful they would be presented by the PD in the same positive light as the Bush dissenters.

Marilyn D. Kopp
Cleveland

The Plain Dealer
Saturday, October 31, 1992

80

Not "Pro-death"

Thank you for your thoughtful coverage of the Aug. 22 pro-life feminist rally. It's time we stop viewing abortion as a woman's right and see it for what it really is: a wrong imposed upon her. Real answers to a woman in a crisis pregnancy lie in eliminating her crisis, not her child.

I was misquoted in the article, however, as saying that not all feminists are "pro-death." We at the National Women's Coalition for Life do not use this term. We don't for a minute believe that any American is "pro-death." We do believe, however, that most Americans are misled and misinformed as to what actually happens in an abortion.

Also misquoted was the number of members in the NWCL. The actual number is 1.8 million. This figure represents six times the membership of the National Organization for Women, which had been previously reported by the PD (June 27) as being the largest women's group in the United States.

Kopp is director of communications for Feminists for Life of Ohio, Greater Cleveland Chapter.

The Plain Dealer
Saturday, September 5, 1992

81

Abortion Battles

Thomas Brazaitis's allegations that President Bush changed his position on population control programs for political expedience ("The real Bush disappeared in 1980," Oct. 27) are unfounded.

In referring to a preface Bush wrote to the 1973 book "World Population Crises: The U.S. Response," Brazaitis omitted a key passage: "But policymaking ... is an educational process. In developing the programs needed, the public as well as government leaders learn from one another. New technologies lead to new policies and laws, new public and private values ... We all proceed by trial and error."

What have we learned in the last 18 years since abortion was legalized? Technological advances in ultrasound and fetal research have offered new insights to our understanding of fetal development and the beginning of human life. These advances have caused many people to reassess the acceptability of the use of abortion in population control programs. Most notable among them is Dr. Bernard Nathanson, one of the founders of the National Abortion Rights Action League and a key activist instrumental in the legalization of abortion in this country. Today he is one of the most prominent and outspoken leaders in the pro-life movement.

Bush has remained consistent in his support of family planning and population control, providing they don't include abortion.

If anything, we've learned that legal abortion hinders the effectiveness of existing birth control programs because its availability deters responsible contraceptive practice. Planned

Parenthood's Alan Guttmacher Research Institute reports that, of the 1.6 million babies killed in abortions each year in the United States, at least 50% of the mothers were using no other form of birth control and more than 40% came back for repeat abortions.

The fact is that not one of the social problems legalized abortion was supposed to improve has gotten better. They have instead gotten dramatically worse. Teenage pregnancy, child abuse and neglect, women and children in poverty, the divorce rate, wife abuse, and the high school dropout rate have all skyrocketed since 1973. A society that tolerates the devaluation of human life through abortion, or in any manner, experiences a lack of respect and protection for human life in all other areas.

Brazaitis falsely concludes that Bush sacrificed personal convictions just to curry favor of "Bible-quoting critics." To the contrary, Bush has remained consistent in personal convictions and open-minded to their growth and development. Brazaitis's "Bible-paranoia" is ironic. Our Constitution borrows from the Bible to protect basic human rights and dignity: "Thou shalt not kill," "Thou shalt not steal," etc. The real question is whether the president should be cowed into abandoning moral responsibilities and values just to appease some misguided liberal critics.

Marilyn D. Kopp
Cleveland

The Plain Dealer
Tuesday, November 19, 1991

82

Why They Rescue

In "Abortion battles" (letters, Nov. 19), Stanley Alprin suggests that, if we outlaw abortion, there will be more babies coming to term. This erroneously assumes there will be as many pregnancies occurring. Evidence indicates otherwise.

In 1978, when welfare funds were cut off, there was a decrease in maternal abortion deaths (legal or illegal), in the total number of abortions, and in the number of live births as well. This decrease in total pregnancies indicates that people are more careful about contraception when abortion is unavailable as a method of birth control.

Pro-lifers are equally concerned about problems of overpopulation and the lack of quality programs for children, but legal abortion only exacerbates these problems. As a national policy, it is both morally repugnant and socially irresponsible.

Marilyn D. Kopp
Cleveland

The Plain Dealer
November 1991

83

Debate over Choice

In a recent letter to the editor, a young woman rejected the viewpoints of three male readers on abortion because of their inability to experience firsthand the dynamics of pregnancy. This sexist bias against men suggests that, because a man has no uterus, he has no rights in determining what happens to his children. It demonstrates a lack of empathy for the profound emotional, intellectual, and spiritual ramifications of what it means to be a father. Many women in our society do not achieve pregnancy because of infertility, menopause, or simply because they don't want to. Does that render their views on abortion invalid as well?

As a mother of two children, I am familiar with the effects of pregnancy on a woman's mind, body, and spirit. They can't compare to the horrendous violence and agony that abortion inflicts on an unborn child.

Outlawing abortion has nothing to do with government forcing women to reproduce. It merely says a woman can't kill the child she has already created. The reader suggests that, if we outlaw abortions, our government could then force women to have them. Can you think of one law that forbids a certain activity but then forces you to engage in it? Before 1973 when abortion was illegal, how many women were forced by our government to have abortions?

The reader's plea "to keep government where it belongs: on Capitol Hill and not in our bedrooms" is also misguided. May I remind her that most abortions are not performed in the bedroom? But even if they were, the bedroom is certainly not exempt from the law. Some of the most heinous crimes serve as an example of the law protecting our society and not invading its privacy.

Since so many of the American people seem to have fallen for this type of double-talk, I shall file the letter under "Doesn't know any better."

Marilyn D. Kopp
Cleveland

The Plain Dealer
Monday, August 5, 1991

PART 2

Articles about Feminists for Life

This section includes articles written about Feminists for Life, reprinted with permission, in different newspaper publications, including the *Free Times*, Cleveland's now-defunct liberal weekly.

84

Agent Provocateur

Her voice is soft, tending toward the meek. It's not what one expects from an agent provocateur. Yet Marilyn Kopp has fashioned a role as a one-woman truth squad for media coverage of the abortion debate. And her beef is this: Cleveland newspapers continue to report that late-term abortions are illegal in Ohio, when it just ain't so.

Kopp's ire was initially sparked in 1998, when then-Judge Patricia Cleary sentenced a pregnant woman to six months in prison, allegedly to prevent her from having an abortion. That, says the Feminists for Life activist, is when the media began reporting that late-term abortions were illegal, though Ohio has no such ban.

As late as December 8, *The Plain Dealer* was still reporting that "Yuriko Kawaguchi did not get out of jail in time to have a legal abortion." Kopp protested, and the error was clarified in a story the next day. But she hasn't had as much luck with the *Free Times*.

In 1999, the alt-weekly reported that "by the time all the legal wrangling came to an end, Kawaguchi was so close to the end of the second trimester that a legal abortion was questionable." Kopp says the paper has continued to leave that impression with readers ever since, despite her letters, which go unprinted, and phone calls, which go unreturned.

Editor Lisa Chamberlain disagrees. She says the use of "questionable" concerned the availability of late-term abortions, not their legality. Besides, the *Free Times* once ran a cover story about the anti-abortion group Feminists for Life's banishment from Lilith Fair and *has* run Kopp's letters before. There's no conspiracy here, says Chamberlain; she's just "not interested in the *Free Times* becoming the Abortion Debate Weekly."

But abortion is a hot topic in the paper, appearing in 51 stories or letters since September 1999. There's plenty of room for debate, counters Kopp, as long as it doesn't include the pro-life viewpoint.

"That's what's especially frustrating," says the self-avowed lefty, who believes she's persona non grata at Cleveland's most left-leaning paper. "Only presenting one perspective is not what lefties are supposed to be about. My main concern is that abortion-choice advocates fought and succeeded in keeping late-term abortions legal, yet repeatedly tell the public they're illegal. They can't have it both ways."

Cleveland Scene
February 15–21, 2001

Note: The Partial-Birth Abortion Ban Act was passed in 2003, prohibiting the procedure in the United States.

85

Lilith Fair Censors Women's Group

Laura DeMarco

No choice. Lilith Fair prides itself on being an inclusive pro-woman event, but apparently their open arms only welcome women who think exactly like them. One feminist group that thought the fair's agenda of raising consciousness and giving them an opportunity to think for themselves recently got an abrupt awakening. Lilith refused to allow national pro-life women's group **Feminists for Life of America** to set up a booth at the traveling convention area that accompanies each concert stop. Only women's groups that espouse a pro-choice point of view, such as NOW and Planned Parenthood, have been given booth space at Lilith (which kicks off July 8 in Vancouver and comes to Blossom on August 17).

"We're threatening to them, apparently," says FFL Ohio Chapter president and national project coordinator **Marilyn Dickstein Kopp**. "I think it's very much at odds with the spirit of inclusivity behind Lilith. The point of Lilith was to give women a voice at concert venues because they were excluded. Now they're giving women a voice, but they're censoring them."

Lilith Fair representatives did not return calls asking for a comment.

No matter what your opinion on the abortion debate, it's shocking that a festival that considers itself pro-woman and pro-choice won't allow opposing voices to be heard or allow women to make up their own minds on the issue. For years, feminists have railed against societal stereotypes. Now they're practicing the same small-mindedness they fought.

No doubt this narrow, close-minded point of view is what led to Lilith's musical domination by safe, middle-brow, middle of the road corporate white folkies.

Cleveland Free Times
July 7–13, 1999

86

GAGGED: Women Behaving Badly in the Women's Movement

Laura DeMarco

Lilith Fair 1999, Blossom Music Center—Women are everywhere. Walking in groups, laughing and talking. Sitting on the grass. Playing the guitar. Reading pamphlets on women's issues picked up from booths in the Village area. Talking reverently about Lilith Fair founder/headlining performer Sarah McLachlan. Waiting in lines at the Tommy Hilfiger table for free samples.

There is also a woman with a gag in her mouth standing in front of one of the booths, sunglasses covering her eyes, her hair pulled back under a baseball cap, her legs rigid and her hands on her hips, wearing a T-shirt reading, "Peace begins in the womb, Sarah."

The woman is Marilyn Kopp, 44, and she's here to make her point: She's been gagged by Lilith Fair, the women's music festival/lifestyle celebration that has dominated the past three concert seasons in the media and at the box office (averaging an impressive $670,000 and 17,000 tickets sold per show in 40 cities this summer).

Kopp is the executive director of the Ohio chapter of Feminists for Life of America, a self-described pro-woman, pro-life activist group that, due to their pro-life politics, was rejected from receiving booth space in the Lilith Fair Village, an area where assorted activists and vendors set up tables to inform/enlighten/sell products. In protest, Kopp and two other FFL members took a different approach this day. They bought tickets, put on gags and assumed their position in front of several pro-choice groups' booths.

In spite of Lilith Fair's lofty goal of wanting to "raise consciousness about issues that affect women's lives," it's apparent not every viewpoint is permitted. The sight of a gagged woman standing in front of a National Organization for Women booth on a day meant to celebrate the female spirit couldn't make this point any clearer.

It also raises some sticky questions. Lilith Fair is much more than a concert and an affirmation of female buying and selling power. With its implied agenda of speaking for and to all women and its predominantly white, middle-class and straight performers and audience, Lilith is a virtual microcosm of the women's movement.

The barring of certain women from Lilith reflects issues affecting the whole movement. What does it mean to be a feminist in 1999? Can you censor other women and be a feminist? Is abortion the litmus test for feminism? Are minorities—racial or ideological—welcome? Are younger women welcome? Do they even want to join? Essentially, is there room for all women in the women's movement?

The Great Abortion Debate

"Hey … How ya doin? … Hi … Hello."

Kopp's words are barely audible—she's got a gag in her mouth—but she's trying her hardest to get her message across to everyone who passes by this hot August day. Some stop, perplexed by the muzzled woman. They get a brief run-down of why Kopp's here. Others give her dirty looks. "I'm with them," a woman shouts, pointing to a Planned Parenthood sign. Another walks up to Kopp, bursts into tears and hugs her. Yet another gets the message totally wrong, from FFL's point of view.

"I thought she was saying she had a choice, that she was with them," says Tina Leonard, gesturing towards the Planned Parenthood booth.

The people at Planned Parenthood don't share her confusion. Most don't even notice Kopp.

"I heard those Feminists for Life were actually buying tickets to come in," says one, laughing. "Sarah'll love that. Good. Give her their money."

Obviously, FFL is not exactly welcome. But why? It's not because of their stance on child support legislation, or their opposition to welfare reform, or their lobbying for the Violence Against Women Act—all causes on which FFL has worked with NOW and Planned Parenthood. FFL isn't wanted because of their position on abortion.

"Their organization says that women shouldn't be allowed to [choose]," explains Lilith head McLachlan, a platinum-selling singer-songwriter and Grammy winner. "I think that's bullshit."

This one issue disqualified the group from the Lilith Village. But do FFL's views on abortion also disqualify them from feminism? It's a tough question. Whether or not pro-life and pro-woman are compatible inspires vehement debate in women's groups, nationally and locally.

"Every person has the right to feel abortion is wrong for their family, but as long as they're trying to impose these views on other people, I don't believe they are feminists," explains Akron NOW President Diane Dodge. "Feminism is choice."

Jackie Hillyer, Ohio NOW president, agrees. "You can be supportive of feminism in certain areas and not others. But whether that makes you a full-fledged feminist is questionable. If you cannot have control of your own life and body, you can't have any control."

Kopp sees things differently.

"Abortion is inconsistent with authentic feminist principles of justice, non-violence and non-discrimination," she says. "Abortion is the ultimate exploitation. It's a symptom of oppression. It's not a solution. We shouldn't have to fit into the model of males for success. I'm pro-human. That's what a feminist is supposed to be."

This has been FFL's view since its beginning in Columbus in 1972, when founder Pat Goltz was expelled from Ohio NOW because she was pro-life, and was soon followed by fellow NOW pro-lifer Catherine Callaghan. The group has been fighting their birth mothers' battle against pro-choice feminism ever since.

The fronts have included Cleveland. Kopp cites an incident that occurred during the mid-90's formation of the Women's Roundtable, a YWCA program that features female speakers at quarterly lunch meetings. There was a great deal of debate as to whether pro-life women should be allowed to participate, though it was eventually decided all women were welcome.

"I'm a strong freedom of choice person, but I respect the rights of women to have other opinions," explains Roundtable chair/lawyer Jan Roller. "People who are anti-choice are welcome. Everyone is welcome. We are not an advocacy group. We do not take a position."

According to Kopp, the organizers of the 1996 Beyond Beijing conference at Cleveland State University weren't so open-minded. She says FFL was initially asked to participate, but she was later told a pro-life side would not be represented. Kopp also claims the group's literature was stolen and their table was trashed at the conference.

It's hard to miss the hypocrisy of feminists censoring other women like this. Not only do such anti-women actions buy into the idea that all women must think the same to belong to the girl's club. The logic behind them patronizingly assumes women aren't smart enough to hear all sides on an issue and decide for themselves.

This view also fails to take into account recent studies, including one by former Planned Parenthood leader Faye Wattleton's Center for Gender Equity, that have found decreased support for abortion rights among women (Wattleton's group found the number of women supporting restrictions on abortion rose from 45 percent in 1997 to 53 percent in 1999). While this study has been dismissed by women's groups simply as evidence that devout and conservative women are becoming more politically vocal, the implication that the beliefs of these women don't matter as much as those of mainstream feminists doesn't diminish the findings. Obviously, not all women do think the same, nor should they have to.

Younger women seem to grasp this idea more readily than their older peers.

Kirsten Rowe, president of the student women's association at CSU, says that although she views reproductive choice as extremely important, the group she leads doesn't expect all women to think like her.

"Any woman with any political belief is welcome," says Rowe. "There's so much focus on diversity and multiculturalism now, people are more considerate of others and their views."

The organizers of Fem Fest, a Cleveland women's music fest that took place the weekend before Lilith, also took such an inclusive approach. They allowed FFL to distribute their literature even though organizer Cathryn Beeks didn't agree with what it said.

"It was a touchy subject, and my first impulse was to not allow them booth space," says Beeks. "But they were very non-confrontational, and their information was important. I didn't see many people interested in the material, but I didn't see many people angry about their presence, either."

The response to Kopp and her crew is the same at Lilith. Many just pass them by; others aim their anger at their silencers.

"I'm pro-choice but I'd like to hear both sides," says Dan Reid, a twentysomething punk (and a rare male to attend Lilith). "I see the one side very well represented here. There are always two sides to an argument. Maybe more."

"Hell … We let the Klan come to Cleveland," exclaims Norma Rodriguez. "Why can't this group talk?"

Mary Marenberg, a pro-choice fortysomething, asks the same question. She doesn't like what FFL has to say, but nor does she like that they aren't allowed to say it.

"It's the same as a pro-choice women's group not being able to speak," she explains.

Some Girls

The parking lot outside Lilith Fair is filled with dependable-looking cars, a necessity for getting to this upscale rural area south of Cleveland.

Closer to the venue, long lines of women shell out $62, $52 or $32 to get in. Almost all of them are white. Almost all of them are well-dressed.. Only the range of ages shows some variety—moms are hanging out with daughters, teens and middle-agers are mixing. The occasional lesbian couple walks by, but it's a rarer sight than you'd expect.

The crowd is the same at the Village area, where, besides the swamped Tommy Hilfiger and Urban Decay makeup booths, the feminist groups represented are predictable: NOW, Planned Parenthood, NARAL, etc. They're all admittedly worthy—and all admittedly establishment. There's no one who might offend or challenge the feminist status quo.

The scene on stage is no more colorful, with middle-of-the-road performers like Sheryl Crow and the Dixie Chicks taking the stage one after another in their designer outfits to play their middlebrow music.

Safe and same are the operative words for the day. They're also two of the criticisms that have dogged the women's movement, which has been derided as primarily by and for middle class, white, professional women. Though this concern doesn't have the high-stakes passion of the abortion debate, it's a more significant and ingrained issue—one that's easy to overlook under all the shouting.

But do these criticisms hold up today? Like Lilith, does the movement still come up with a prohibitively high price and a platform that only speaks to some?

No, according to members of NOW, the leading voice in the feminist establishment, which has become nearly synonymous with the women's movement, in part due to the 33-year-old group's historical significance and in part due to the well-funded organization assuming the role of speaking for all women.

"I have heard criticisms of NOW since 1972, but I never believed it was an ingrained part of our organization," says Dodge. "It was just that in the early '60s, when NOW was beginning, the reality was that it was white women who had been staying at home with their children who had the available time and funds. There will always be individual problems where a minority may not feel welcome, but overall NOW is very accepting."

Hillyer cites outreach programs for minorities and young feminists as signs that the group is now more welcoming than ever.

But is this really the case? Even if groups such as NOW do have open doors, do all women want to walk through them? NOW has seen a steady decrease in membership since the ERA heyday of the early '80s. Cleveland used to have both

East and West Side chapters, but now doesn't even have one. Womenspace, an umbrella organization for Cleveland women's groups since 1975, died due to lack of interest in 1995.

This is partly a sign of a general diversification in society. Niche groups for black women, or lesbians, or Republican women, or women who want to focus their energy on reproductive rights, have drawn members from organizations like NOW, as have other general-interest, often local, women's groups.

Another reason for the decline can be traced to the White House.

"When Clinton was elected, the perception was [that] all was well. He would protect us," explains Hillyer. "There was less fear of losing reproductive rights and activism became less."

Clinton also hurt the women's movement in more straightforward ways. Women's groups enamored by his ardent pro-choice politics seem to have made a trade-off with the president, ignoring his actions (policy and personal) on other issues since he gave them this break. But overlooking the fact that the great protector is also a great womanizer—even when that womanizing included an intern putting out for the boss and getting a great job for her efforts—highlighted the hypocrisy in the established women's movement, giving fuel to its detractors and turning off many more thoughtful or moderate women.

But to completely blame the shrinking of old-school feminism on splinter groups or Bill Clinton doesn't address a core issue. Despite its claims of remaining relevant, the establishment doesn't speak for, or listen to, many women.

This is increasingly visible on a socioeconomic level. Though women from lower economic classes have historically had neither the time or money to join women's groups—though they may support them in principle—recent years have seen a number of set-backs affecting lower-class women, such as welfare reform. Most have been met with near silence from the feminist masses, whose stock portfolios are riding high on the good-time economic wave. And the brutal treatment Paula Jones received at the mouths of many in the women's movement only reinforced its image as elitist. Despite NOW President Patricia Ireland's assertion that her lack of support for Jones was based on her ties to right-wing groups, not her big hair, the message sent to poor women was loud and clear: "trailer trash" not welcome.

Racial minorities have received a warmer welcome. "NOW made an intense effort in the '80s, as far as affirmative action goes. Each region now has at least one woman of color representative," explains Hillyer in reference to initiatives NOW instituted to raise minority membership.

But even with such programs, many minorities don't want to join NOW.

Thirty-three-year-old Michelle McDonald, an African-American woman who came to Lilith Fair with three white friends, explains why. She said she'd feel as out of place in NOW as she did at the concert.

"They don't talk about things that matter to me. You always see white women on TV representing these groups," she says. "As a black woman, [the women's movement] is not about my life."

Gestures towards sexual minorities by NOW are often met with a similar lack of interest, particularly among younger, more radical lesbians.

Terry and Jo (they don't want their last names used), a couple who came to the concert "just for fun," say they'd be more likely to join a gay and lesbian group that included men than a women-only organization.

"They address concerns that more directly affect our lives," explains Terry.

The description of the women's movement as "not about my life" also echoes loudly among a segment of the population women's groups are trying desperately to attract: women under 30. Though groups have undertaken extensive efforts to attract younger women to their graying ranks, they have largely failed.

"It's a sign of the times," explains Roller. "The struggles of '70s were successful somewhat, and young women don't see the need."

But according to women like 26-year-old Rowe, it's not that younger women don't see the need. It's that they don't see what *they* need in old-school feminist groups.

"I went to a NOW meeting," she says. "It was filled with older women, and I had a really hard time relating to their issues."

Her experience is typical. Rowe's words reverberate from others across the Lilith Fair lawn, like 22-year-old Trina Evans. "I've never even thought about joining [a women's group]. That's more for people my mom's age," says Evans.

So what issues are younger women interested in?

It's a tricky question. In part, the difference has to do with emphasis. Younger women cite topics such as date rape, violence against women and reproductive choice as most relevant to their lives, while their older counterparts seem more concerned with equality in the workplace and children-related issues—though they too cite the topics younger women mention as significant.

The real generational disconnect has more to do with attitude than issues. Ironically, this may be a sign of the women's movement's success. As Rowe explains, "A lot of [young women] don't want to be associated with feminism. But you ask what they think of equal pay or of choice, and they're all for it. They just don't equate those issues with feminism."

Equality is something young women take for granted (though most realize we haven't reached some utopian state). From this perspective, many feminists seem like bitter war-horses fighting yesterday's battle and expecting all other women to follow their rigid code of acceptable actions. Feminism itself seems an outdated movement that still perceives women as victims, not the bastion of equality those within its walls believe it to be.

This is not necessarily negative, however. The inherent sense of equality young women possess may allow them to be more pro-woman than their mothers—whether or not they label themselves feminist. Since they don't have to constantly band together to fight for equal rights, they're freer to act as individuals. They're also more willing to allow others to do the same, even ideological rebels like FFL, the true minorities who have been gagged by this movement where diversity is often skin deep.

The picture's not completely rosy—many younger women enjoy inherited equality but want it just for women like them—but the signs suggest change is coming. Groups like CSU's student women's association that welcome women of all colors, ages, religions, classes and places on the political spectrum are replacing NOW branches on college campuses. The riot girl punk movement has provided a rebellious, anarchic, and *fun* balance to the dour establishment for the past decade, proving you don't have to wear your agenda on your sleeve to prove you've got girl power. Pro-sex, pro-girl, anti-PC magazines like *Bust* are burying publications like *Ms.* at the newsstand. Younger generations seem less willing to partake in the reverse sexism of their forerunners, though issues like increasing suicide rates among teenage boys are still often ignored by feminists who only seem concerned about helping girls deal with their inner Ophelia. Camile Paglia suggests younger women are happier to—if not embrace—at least cohabitate with all of their sisters.

Witness this scene from Lilith Fair. As Kopp cohort Denise Mackura stands gagged in front of the NOW booth, a group of teenage girls walk up to her. When they find out what's going on, they're shocked. They see the situation as a violation of civil rights, not a defense of women's rights.

"This is wrong," says Casey Patton, 17.

It's a simple declaration, but like Kopp's willingness to fight for her rights, it's a much more feminist statement than the one made by Sheryl Crow earlier in the day.

"This isn't a democracy. This is a tyranny," said Crow, justifying Lilith's ban on pro-life groups.

But do her words describe only Lilith Fair? They will if women like Kopp and those who speak up for her have their say. Whether or not the women's movement has room for them doesn't matter. They're making their own space. That's empowerment.

Cleveland Free Times
September 22–28, 1999

(See letter 52, "Praise for DeMarco," in part 1)

87

The Year of Women in Rock?
Don't Believe the Hype, Baby

Laura DeMarco

Lilith Fair would have you believe it. So would VH-1. Even the *Billboard* charts seem to support it.

But don't believe the hype. This is not the year of Women in Rock.

Just look at the giant frat party called *Woodstock*, where eight alleged rapes were reported, including two in the mosh pit during sets by testosterone rockers Limp Bizkit and Korn. Where Sheryl Crow was greeted with screams to show her breasts.

Or look at the Vans Warped Tour. Once punk stood for equality and open-mindedness. But today's neo-punks are neo-Neanderthals. With almost no female performers, Vans was dominated by jocks' antics. Performers taunted girls in the audience with lewd remarks. In more than one city, Blink-182's Mark Hoppus invited women in the crowd to come up onstage and satisfy his bandmates. At the Cleveland show, hordes of teenage boys egged on girls to take off their tops at the "What Would You Do For a Yoohoo" booth. Sure haven't come a long way baby.

Ironically, Lilith hasn't helped the cause. On the surface, the self-congratulatory fem-fest seems to be a bold step forward. Under the directorship of one female singer-songwriter, Sarah McLachlan, a bunch of female artists got together and created one of the most financially successful tours in years. These sisters are doing it for themselves.

But that's part of the problem. They seem to be doing it *just* for themselves, or for other women just like them. They've broken down the barriers to the boys' club and have created an equally exclusive girls' club. Though this year's tour shows some broadening with the addition of artists like R&B diva Deborah Cox and the country Dixie Chicks to the previously almost all-white, neo-folkie bill, it's a false diversity. Under their varied colors and sounds, these women are all the same— middlebrow, middle-of-the-road performers on labels with enough clout to muscle them onto a sought-after tour slot. Only the inclusion of unrepentantly anti-PC punk godmother Chrissie Hyde showed some daring. True to form, Hyde had the guts to call the tour what it was ("The fact that it's all women is just a gimmick," Hyde told *Rolling Stone*) and still take advantage of it. But where are the other punks and riot girls, blues mamas, avant-garders, old-school country gals, metal chicks and hip-hop poets?

Probably back home, struggling to make it from the grassroots up. But this is not to say that they deserve some kind of sympathy because they're women. They're as capable as any man of working their way up.

The real problem with the absence of women like these on Lilith is the message it sends. Lilith celebrates female performers for being pretty, earnest and flowery—perhaps political on "women's issues," but not political enough to threaten. Take the controversy earlier this year when women's group Feminists for Life was refused a booth at the Lilith village because of its pro-life stance. Instead of assuming today's women are empowered enough to hear all sides of an issue and make their own decision, Lilith kept FFL away. Men have been censoring women for years, but now women are doing it to themselves. Lilith may be safer than Woodstock for members of the female gender, but "safe" has become the operative word—safe politics, safe performers, safe music.

Thus Lilith-like performers are ghettoized as "women's acts" who play their girly music on the girls' stage, mostly just for girls. The music world is more segregated than ever, with macho rockers like Limp Bizkit on one side and pretty fluff like Jewel on the other. And women who don't fit the Lilith mode aren't invited onto the girls' *or* boys' stage. Where were the women at Vans? Off to the side, shaking their tits for a chocolate drink.

Except for L7. These riot rockers showed the crowds at Vans, and Lilith, what women can really do—without playing a note. The L.A. group hired a plane to fly over Lilith with a banner reading "Bored? Tired? Try L7." Vans fans were greeted with the message that "Warped needs more beaver" (the plane company wouldn't fly the original message, "Warped needs more pussy"). Now that's empowerment.

But what about those who say even the girls at Vans are empowered? It's their choice to strip. Or what about the fact that women are selling more records than ever? Isn't VH-1's much hyped tribute to the "100 Greatest Women of Rock" a sign of how far women have come?

There's some truth to these arguments. But not as much as a glance suggests. Sure, these girls are choosing to take their shirts off, and Britney Spears allegedly chose to have her breasts enlarged. But she didn't choose the factors that made it lucrative for a teenage performer to have big breasts. And those boys at Vans weren't gawking at the size of a girl's empowerment. And sure, women are selling well, but except for the occasional Lauryn Hill, today's chart toppers are either teen queens (Britney, Spice Girls), bad-ass, self-degrading sex pots (Foxy Brown, L'il Kim) or plastic dolls (Mariah, Shania, Jewel).

And while it was certainly amusing to watch VH-1 and figure out why Carly Simon ranks higher than Joan Jett, who ranks better than Cher, who beats Kate Bush and Siouxsie Sioux, this kind of list-making is more an affirmation of female buying power than musical strength.

So when Lilith and her exclusive assembly of sisters roll into town this week, don't be fooled. Call 1999 what it is: the year of some women in rock, sometimes.

Cleveland Free Times
August 11–17, 1999

88

Prolife Feminism: Yesterday and Today

*Rachel MacNair, Mare Krane Derr, and Linda Naranjo-Huebl,
editors*
Sulzberger & Graham

Kathy Ewing

To most of us, "pro-life feminism" is an oxymoron. We've encountered two sides to the abortion issue in the media, and feminists line up uniformly on the pro-choice side.

The editors of *Prolife Feminism* have complicated this simplistic view by reprinting dozens of essays—some by early feminists, others more recent—that see a logical connection between prolife and feminist attitudes. More precisely, they see a logical connection between abortion and the oppression of women.

All the famous foremothers are here: Elizabeth Cady Stanton, Susan B. Anthony, Victoria Woodhull (the first woman to run for president), Sylvia Pankhurst (a renowned pacifist and suffragist), and many others. To a woman, they rail against solving a "problem" with violence, letting men off the hook, and picking on beings weaker than ourselves.

The contemporary writers are a varied lot. Many preach a "social feminism," which argues that society needs to become more accepting of women and children. "Accepting short term solutions like abortion only delays the implementation of real reforms like decent maternity and paternity leave, job protection, (and) high-quality childcare …," says Daphne Clair de Jong, a New Zealand writer. Many belong to Feminists for

163

Life of America, a prolife group ignored by the media because of its calm and conciliatory voice.

One of the most affecting pieces is Elizabeth McAlister's "Letter from a Women's Prison," composed when McAlister (married to peace activist Philip Berrigan) was serving a two-year prison sentence for destroying equipment used for carrying nuclear weapons at an Air Force base. She was responding to a full-page letter in the *New York Times* from Catholics for a Free Choice. She asks them not to let the Moral Majority, Ronald Reagan, Jerry Falwell and many Catholic bishops frame the argument—"cherishing the unborn even while they damn the born to the Gehenna of war, violence, social and personal neglect."

She continues, "I think our task implies something more difficult, more imaginative, than merely responding in kind. We must widen the frame. We must stretch our arms and our hearts until we include and cherish every human aspiration, every endangered or despised or expendable life. In such ways, we do great service, both to church and state."

By connecting issues of peace and non-violence to abortion, McAlister presents a challenging alternative to the acrimonious, two-sided debate so familiar to us all.

Cleveland Free Times
Wednesday, March 6, 1996

89

FFL-Ohio Sponsors Controversial Art Show

Serrin Foster
President, Feminists for Life of America

Note: In 1994, Feminists for Life of Ohio sponsored an art and poetry exhibit at a gallery in Cleveland. I first learned of artist Mary Cate Carroll and her controversial painting "American Liberty Upside Down" while reading Nat Hentoff's book "Free Speech for Me—But Not for Thee." I contacted Hentoff, and he told me how to get in touch with the artist. I came up with the idea to have an exhibit with Carroll's artwork and hand-calligraphied poetry by Jean Blackwood, a consistent-ethic-of-life advocate. It took a year and a half to find an art gallery that was willing to exhibit the show. Carroll is a Christian artist whose work reflects a deep spirituality and concern for justice. Blackwood had been influenced by Zen Buddhism and Taoism. In keeping with her philosophy of "do no harm," she is an animal rights activist and vegetarian. Both Carroll and Blackwood, while starting from different perspectives, addressed similar issues: inclusivity, social justice, spirituality, and nonviolence. The following article describing the controversy, written by Feminists for Life's president Serrin Foster, was printed in FFL's biannual magazine The American Feminist.*

An artist's work is on exhibit for the first time in the almost 10 years since her depiction of an aborted child as a martyr to "modern convenience" was censored in 1983.

"BEcause ... a cause for BEing" features the work of Maryland artist Mary Cate Carroll, whose painting from the series "American Liberty Upside Down" was banned at Mary

Washington College for its portrayal of an unborn baby as a martyr enshrined in a modern rendition of a medieval tomb.

Poet Jean Blackwood's writings from her anthology *Beyond Beginning and Other Poems* are also exhibited throughout the display at the Idea Garage, a gallery in the heart of Cleveland's cultural center, Oct. 21 to Nov. 21.

Feminists for Life of Ohio is sponsoring the exhibit "to explore the concept of feminism as human rights advocacy, especially stressing the relationship between women's rights and issues of peace, equality, and justice," chapter president Marilyn Kopp said.

Ms. Carroll drew upon her fascination with reliquaries to create the controversial piece. A reliquary enshrines the remains of part or all of a human being, usually a martyr. During the Middle Ages, the human remains were carried through the streets in solemn processions.

Ms. Carroll created a modern-day reliquary for an aborted five-month-old fetus she named Johnny Doe. The child was "not one killed for his beliefs, but one killed because his life was deemed inconvenient," Ms. Carroll said recently in an interview with *The American Feminist*. She gave Johnny "a voice, a recourse to protest, that was denied him under 'the law' at the time of his death," the artist said.

"I have introduced the victim into the conversation."

Johnny is preserved in a bottle of formaldehyde, hidden by a door in an almost cartoonish painting of two parents holding a child. Ms. Carroll believes when the viewer chooses to open the door "Johnny speaks more effectively than any artist or writer could."

Free speech advocate Nat Hentoff reported on the debate over the painting's censorship through a series of articles in the *Village Voice* after Mary Washington College censored the painting in 1983. Ms. Carroll was told initially that her painting was too "controversial" and "inappropriate" for a college art show, and "in poor taste," Mr. Hentoff noted.

Ironically, the pro-choice chair of the Fredericksburg, VA, college art department, Prof. Barbara Meyer, said the work demonstrated a lack of respect for human life by the artist.

"Had we allowed the flagrant and crass exploitation of this pathetic form, we would have flouted a moral as well as a legal obligation to treat it with dignity." Ms. Meyer said.

"Reverence for life is an essential component of the human condition," the professor told the *Fredericksburg Free Lance-Star* in 1984.

Later, Ms. Carroll was told the artwork was banned because it would violate a Virginia law that prohibited transporting dead human bodies over state lines for purposes other than "the lawful exhibition for scientific education and training in health and related subjects."

After a two-year legal battle, the Maryland artist and the college settled out of court. She was invited back to display the piece and her legal costs were paid. Ms. Carroll won the fight for Johnny Doe to finally be heard ... by finally being seen.

The Plain Dealer's art critic, Steven Litt, wrote an unflattering review of the exhibit. I submitted the following letter to the Plain Dealer *in response, but it was never published:*

In response to Steven Litt's review of the art and poetry exhibit at the Idea Garage (Banned art takes center stage, Nov. 14) sponsored by Feminists for Life:

Litt dismissed the controversial abortion painting by Baltimore artist Mary Cate Carroll (and thereby the entire exhibit) as nothing more than "publicity art" designed to generate media coverage. Would Litt then reject the use of art to graphically address other political issues as well, such as AIDS, domestic violence, or breast cancer? Or is public consciousness-raising only legitimate if one happens to agree with the particular perspective being presented?

Litt argued that the abortion painting was the only reason the exhibit existed, but it was Litt, not Feminists for Life, who singled out the abortion piece. He completely disregarded the entire body of work by the other artist in the show, Colorado poet Jean Blackwood, who performed two readings at the opening reception and whose work was displayed in hand-calligraphied book format on pedestals throughout the gallery.

In an attempt to portray the exhibit as a self-promoting publicity stunt, Litt disingenuously called attention to a literature table in the gallery with a sign asking for contributions. He failed to mention (as the sign explicitly stated) the contributions were for a local battered women's shelter and a local pregnancy care center, not for Feminists for Life.

These and other omissions were misleading. The exhibit was designed to examine the concept of feminism as human rights advocacy. The title of the exhibit, "BEcause ... a cause for BEing," was never even mentioned in the review. Contrary to Litt's claim that the entire show was built around Carroll's painting (and as the photos accompanying the review helped demonstrate), the two artists explored a wide range of issues: women's place(s) in society, spirituality, social justice and nonviolence.

While the abortion piece may have been unsettling, it was actually another painting, "Feminist Icon," from the same series that commanded more attention because of its audio elements. It depicted a woman dressed in business attire sitting at a desk surrounded by diplomas on the wall. In her middle was a door (where her heart would be), which, when pulled open, emitted a loud, blood-curdling woman's scream.

Litt's inability to relate to Carroll's relief sculptures, which he described as "pencil drawings" depicting "an anorexic female nude undergoing a variety of torments," was perhaps due to his inability to personally experience the same kinds of societal pressures and expectations (sometimes subtle, sometimes blatant) that women encounter.

This might be particularly true in the case of abortion, where the pressures and expectations are often brought upon by men. As French pro-choice feminist Simone de Beauvoir noted in her book "The Second Sex," "It is often the seducer himself who convinces the woman that she must rid herself of the child. Or he may have already abandoned her.... Men tend to take abortion lightly; they regard it as one of the numerous hazards imposed on women by malignant nature, but fail to realize fully the values involved."

Carroll's work, however, dealt not just with victimization and oppression as Litt noted; her search for God reflected fortitude, perseverance, and faith as well.

"BEcause ... a cause for BEing" was, in essence, about wounds to the human spirit and the struggle to be whole. It was about not looking the other way (or to paraphrase Blackwood, to remain "all shut and safe and forgetting to grow"). Or, "assuming justice is our business," we can be called to a deeper level of compassion and work toward the day "when choices belong not only to the strong."

The choice is up to each of us.

Marilyn D. Kopp
Cleveland

I am president of Feminists for Life of Ohio.

90

Feminists for Life Key on Pro-life Agenda

Janet O'Donnell

When her daughter was born three years ago, Jean Graham of Lakewood decided she should get interested in women and their thinking.

Among the issues that affected women was abortion, something she had always opposed but without any clear-cut rationale.

In her reading, she came across the book *Completely Pro-Life.*

"Ron Sider said in the book that you can't call yourself pro-life unless you have a consistent attitude against war, capital punishment, tobacco and other things that kill people."

About the same time she heard about Feminists for Life, a national organization started in Columbus in 1972 by two women who were expelled from the National Organization for Women because of their pro-life views.

Graham had never before joined any pro-life organization but this group's mission of advocating for women in all areas of life appealed to her.

So, the college English professor joined the national organization of Feminists for Life and formed the Cleveland chapter. She now serves as vice president of Feminists for Life of Ohio, which has about 200 members statewide, and is coordinator for the Cleveland area.

Shortly after, Marilyn Kopp of Cleveland heard about Feminists for Life at a Jan. 22 pro-life rally.

"It immediately struck me what a powerful argument their message was," she said.

At a time in history when feminism seems synonymous with pro-abortion, Kopp said she learned that the roots of feminism are planted deeply in opposition to abortion.

"Yes, the early feminists in this country were strongly pro-life," explained the professional map maker who is also director of communications for Feminists for Life of Ohio.

Women like Susan B. Anthony, Elizabeth Cady Stanton, and Victoria Woodhull spoke strongly against abortion more than century ago. "These women were very progressive thinkers," said Kopp.

"They believed that all human persons had an equal claim to basic human rights and dignity. They also believed that abortion was not a solution to inequality but a symptom of it."

Quoting an 1873 letter from Stanton to social reformer Julia Ward Howe, Kopp said, "When we consider that women are treated as property, it is degrading to women that we should treat our children as property to be disposed of as we see fit." [See footnote on letter number 34.]

Feminists for Life, Kopp and Graham explained, is based on the premise that women must be working to transform society to create a world that recognizes the inherent worth of all human beings.

Kopp explained that Feminists for Life promotes that it is "inconsistent to demand rights for ourselves and to deny them to the unborn."

After all, she notes, some of those unborn people are women too.

The argument that women should have a right to choose what to do with their own bodies does not promote equality, Kopp added. Instead, it liberates men from responsibility for their behavior as well as financial and emotional responsibility for their children.

Among the goals of the organization is to encourage

women to become educated in pregnancy and childbirth and to work toward alleviating the problems in society that cause women to seek abortions.

"Women should be working together for women," Kopp said.

She said she finds pain in "the divisiveness of the issue." For that reason, she is enthusiastic about the group's Common Ground approach to working with other women's organizations.

Common Ground, Graham explained, is a movement that came together "spontaneously," joining activists on both sides of the abortion issue to promote common goals.

Among those goals is providing a support network for pregnant women, fostering gender awareness, providing aid to women and children, and facilitating adoption for those who seek it.

"We have to recognize that being pro-life should not end at birth."

For that reason, she said the national organization of Feminists for Life is working in conjunction with the National Organization for Women to lobby support for the Violence Against Women Act.

"If it passes we believe it will reduce the number of abortions because women can more easily avoid abusive relationships," she said.

Feminists for Life is working on the Real Choices research project, listening to women who have had abortions to learn the reasons why. The group has also sponsored a candlelight vigil against the death penalty as well as Project Preemie Togs to provide neonatal units with tiny garments for premature infants.

Feminists for Life is also one of the sponsors of the

Consistent Ethic of Life seminar from 2–5 p.m. Oct. 3 at St. Ignatius of Antioch Church in Cleveland.

Women, Kopp said, should not be forced to choose whether to carry their pregnancies to term.

"In order to be equal we shouldn't have to change our bodies—to undergo surgery. We have to work for equal opportunities for women, for equal pay for equal work. We have to view child-bearing as evidence of women's tremendous power.

"Ours is a celebrational feminism that recognizes the inherent differences of the sexes and finds each equally valuable."

For more information, call 216-4612 or (513) 845-1241.

O'Donnell is a freelance writer from North Olmsted.

Catholic Universe Bulletin
September 24, 1993

91

Drawing a New Line

Mark Naymik

Cleveland is once again being targeted by an anti-abortion group as part of a nationwide campaign to stop abortions. But this group, National Women's Coalition for Life (NWCL), which will visit Cleveland on September 7 as part of a 12-city tour, isn't preparing to link arms and block access to abortion clinics, raise signs, or even organize a rally. NWCL says it plans just to talk to women who have had abortions.

"We want to get a better handle on what leads women to have an abortion and come up with practical suggestions for alternatives," says Frederica Mathewes-Green, director of the NWCL-sponsored research project called *Real Choices*, which will center around small focus groups with women who have had abortions and say they regret having had them.

Mathewes-Green, the current vice president for Feminists for Life of America who once advocated abortion as an important element of women's rights, says that NWCL wants to use the research findings to fight the abortion battle on a practical level and not a political one. "We are not concerned to make abortion illegal.... We are not going to go to Capitol Hill and yell abortion kills babies.... The political world is too transitory and it is not where we want to put our trust."

Mathewes-Green will travel to all 12 cities—including Chicago, Washington, Los Angeles, Jacksonville, Phoenix, Boston, New York, and Pittsburgh—beginning with Cleveland to conduct the focus groups and solicit input from crisis center personnel and abortion providers in order to answer the question "What would it have taken for a woman who has

174

had an abortion to have chosen life?" Mathewes-Green says she expects to complete the tour by the end of April.

"Through this project we want to examine very specifically what life crises like school and economics made these women feel like they had to have an abortion, and develop solutions that eliminate the pressures," says Mathewes-Green. She says NWCL is planning on publishing the findings in a book to be out sometime next year.

NWCL, which was founded only 18 months ago, is a network of more than 15 national women's groups that oppose abortion and boasts a combined membership of 1.8 million. While its member groups are diverse—from Women for Women to American Victims of Abortion to Professional Women's Network—and vary widely on women's issues, NWCL executive director Jeannie French says the coalition's members are "united on the abortion issue."

According to French, Cleveland is included in the *Real Choices* project because "it has a healthy potential for reasonable dialogue." Marilyn Kopp of Greater Cleveland's chapter of Feminists for Life of Ohio is coordinating the research locally for NWCL and will be working with Mathewes-Green. Kopp says she is optimistic that Cleveland will come up with practical solutions to counter pressures some women who choose abortion face. "Cleveland has the reputation for doing more than just talking," she says.

Cleveland Free Times
August 25, 1993

PART 3

Summaries of Articles about Feminists for Life

In addition to the op-eds and letters I have written, several other articles about Feminists for Life's activities have been published. This section will summarize some of these articles, in accordance with the Fair Use Doctrine.

92

In "Giving pregnant students a place to turn" (February 29, 2000), Michele M. Melendez of the *Plain Dealer* described Feminists for Life's College Outreach Program, which addresses the needs of pregnant and parenting students on college campuses.

The program also lobbies for services such as housing for pregnant and parenting students, on-site day care, adoption counseling, and maternity coverage in student health care plans.

The article included information about the Pregnancy Resource Forum at Kent State University moderated by FFL's national president, Serrin Foster, and brought together key campus policymakers and stakeholders to identify and develop resources for pregnant and parenting students.

As Elizabeth Quinn, vice president of Kent's Campus Right to Life group, which co-sponsored the event, said, "When a college student gets pregnant, people automatically assume she'll have to drop out or get an abortion. All we want to do is talk about that."

93

Rachel MacNair, past president of Feminists for Life of America, edited an excellent and instructive book, "Prolife Feminism: Yesterday and Today." The book was reviewed in the *Plain Dealer* by Rebecca Freligh in a January 23, 1996, article, "Feminist essays support all life."

The book is a series of pro-life essays written by our feminist foremothers, including Susan B. Anthony, Elizabeth Cady Stanton, and Victoria Claflin Woodhull. This collection also included essays by contemporary pro-life feminists such as Daphne Clair de Jong and Frederica Mathewes-Green.

In her review of the book, Freligh quoted me as saying that none of the modern feminists I've encountered were aware that the founders of the feminist movement who wrote about abortion were, without known exception, pro-life, as illustrated by the essays in MacNair's book. Freligh quoted my statement: "Without a firm understanding of where we've come from, it's difficult to have a clear vision of where we need to go."

In her article, Freligh quoted de Jong from her essay "Feminism and Abortion: The Great Inconsistency." In her essay, de Jong wrote, "The feminist claim to equality is based on the equal rights of all human beings. The most fundamental of all is the right to life. If women are to justify taking this right from the unborn, they must contend that their own superiority of size, of power, or of physique or intellect or need, or their own value as a person, transcends any right of the unborn. In the long history of male chauvinism, all these have been seen as good reasons for withholding human rights from women."

Freligh's review of the book was thorough and well written. I strongly encourage readers to check out the book.

94

Another article was also published in the *Plain Dealer* on January 23, 1996, by Rebecca Freligh, "Both sides find common ground 23 years after Roe." Most of the article identifies areas of common ground between pro-life and pro-choice proponents but also highlights their stark differences on abortion.

Areas in which both sides work together include Common Ground dialogue groups; lobbying against welfare reform legislation that would have penalized mothers on welfare who bring more children into the world; and working together to successfully pass the Violence Against Women Act. This bipartisan legislation responds to issues of domestic violence, sexual assault, dating violence, and stalking.

Additionally, Feminists for Life is concerned that abortion will be promoted as a remedy for problems faced by low-income women. She quotes me as saying, "Certainly, if women feel compelled to abort for economic reasons, they are not making free choices."

The article concludes with a statement from the ACLU's Reproductive Freedom Project reaffirming their commitment to, and defense of, abortion rights.

95

Common Ground on abortion is a concept that attempts to bring together those on opposite sides of the debate to respectfully dialogue and to identify areas of mutual concern that they can work on together to help women and children, such as adoption or preventing teen pregnancy. (See the article I wrote about it, number 76, "Uncommon Cause, Common Ground.)

The Cleveland Common Ground group was formed as a result of a 1993 forum sponsored by the local chapter of Feminists for Life. Because of my involvement with Common Ground, I was invited to join the national steering committee of the Common Ground Network for Life and Choice in Washington, DC. The committee was made up of representatives from different Common Ground groups across the country. I served on the committee for three and a half years.

Common Ground generated much media coverage, but the most in-depth article was a cover story by Joe Frolik in the August 13, 1995, Sunday Magazine section of the Cleveland *Plain Dealer*, "On the Abortion Battleground, Some Warriors Are Finding COMMON GROUND."

This article contains an interesting discussion on the challenges and emotions associated with getting a group of people together who maintain strongly held, opposing views on abortion (i.e., "baby killers" versus "oppressors of women"). The process is not for everyone because, sometimes, the core beliefs on both sides are too strong to allow people to look for common ground on abortion. Pro-choicers would say that, if women cannot control decisions over whether and when to have children, they cannot control their lives. But pro-lifers counter that abortion is simply another form of violence against women—and children, too.

The article notes that, if you believe your opponent has diametrically opposing views and is evil, there isn't a need for civility. However, it suggests that, if you are willing to do the hard work of listening and discussing instead of demonizing, over time you just might find some common ground.

<h1 style="text-align:center">96</h1>

Rebecca Freligh wrote an article for the *Plain Dealer* titled "Feminists for Life—Group wants a common ground to talk out its differences with women who advocate abortion rights." It was published on November 23, 1993.

Jean Graham, a member of Feminists for Life of Ohio, wrote a letter to the editor titled "Women still a long way from justice" in response to Rebecca Freligh's article. It was published in the *Plain Dealer* on January 5, 1994.

To summarize the article and letter, many women have a deep desire for gender parity—that is, "the equality and full humanity of women and men." Rachel MacNair, the national president for Feminists for Life at the time, said, "We dynamite the very foundations of feminism if we take any group of human beings and put them outside the realm of protection." Dr. Alice Bunker Stockham, a family planning advocate, wrote that the woman undergoing an abortion "risks her own life and health in the act, and commits the highest crime in the calendar, for she takes the life of her own child. She defrauds the child of the right to existence."

An Oberlin history professor, Carol Lasser, claimed that the early feminists were pro-motherhood. However, Jean Graham and I claimed that the early feminists supported a woman's right to choose motherhood, as well as her right to use contraception. These early feminists "blamed men for enforced maternity," and they blamed men for enforced abortions. So why do women choose to have an abortion? The major reasons are difficulty of adoption, an absent or unsupportive partner, and the inability to afford a child.

The first feminists were pioneers in expanding women's roles; they included the first female graduates in medicine, law, and religion. They were instrumental in numerous areas of social change, including abolition, the anti-war movement, and birth control. Even with these positive changes, there is still a double standard in society that says a woman can achieve equality only by undergoing an invasive surgery that destroys her child. This is not a price men pay for sex. Abortion is another example of how deeply ingrained sexism is in our culture and an indication of how far women still need to go to achieve justice and equal rights.

97

An article titled "Abortion issue divides 2 rallying feminist groups" by Harry Stainer was published in the *Plain Dealer* on Sunday, August 23, 1992. In it, Stainer wrote about a pro-choice feminist rally and a pro-life feminist rally that were held in downtown Cleveland on the same day.

The pro-choice rally was sponsored by the Greater Cleveland chapter of the National Organization for Women (NOW), the National Abortion Rights Action League, Womenspace, Hard Hatted Women, the Cleveland Rape Crisis Center, Planned Parenthood of Greater Cleveland, and the Socialist Worker's Party. Democratic state senator Eric Fingerhut and Barbara Otto from 9to5 were among the speakers.

At the pro-life rally, speakers included women from the National Women's Coalition for Life, Feminists for Life, the Professional Women's Network, and Women Exploited by Abortion (WEBA). Pro-life women held signs that read "Peace in the Womb," "Equal pay for equal work," and "Not NOW, not ever."

The two rallies demonstrated the diversity of views women have on the abortion issue. (See my letter about the rallies, number 80 "Not 'Pro-death.'")

CONCLUSION

In conclusion, I would like to share the transcript of a speech I gave, "Reclaiming Our Past, Creating a Future," on July 19, 1998, at the "Celebrate '98" gathering in Seneca Falls, New York, to commemorate the 150th anniversary of the first Women's Rights Convention, which marked the beginning of organized feminism in the United States. Three hundred women and men attended the original Seneca Falls convention, which was organized by Elizabeth Cady Stanton, Lucretia Mott, Mary Ann M'Clintock, Martha Coffin Wright, and Jane Hunt. These women were also active in the abolitionist movement to end slavery and racial discrimination but became disaffected by its failure to include women as equals. The "Declaration of Sentiments," written primarily by Stanton and adopted at that historic 1848 gathering, contained many demands for women's equality, including (by a slim margin because it was so controversial) women's right to vote. It wouldn't be until 1920, after a seventy-five-year battle, that women were finally granted political enfranchisement—the right to vote.

> Thank you. It's great to be back in New York. I was just in Rochester last weekend as part of the Feminists for Life protest at the national NOW convention. For those of you who hadn't heard, we dressed in suffragist costumes and handed out literature about the pro-woman, pro-life views of the feminist foremothers whom we honor this week at Celebrate '98. We also wore gags over our mouths to protest NOW's expulsion of pro-life feminists from

their ranks and NOW's attempts to censor our views on why early feminist opposition to abortion is relevant today. Well, as you may have noticed, today the gags are off.

My eight- and ten-year-old daughters came with me, and as we were changing into our suffragist outfits in the restroom of the hotel lobby where NOW held its convention, we were surprised to discover all the new best friends we had made—NOW members from across the country who were excited to see us in our costumes, thrilled that we would come from so far away to participate, until of course they realized that we were going to protest abortion outside. Then we rather quickly and mysteriously contracted leprosy, as they refused to speak to us any further!

Two other women from Ohio that I know and admire a great deal had a similar experience back in 1972. Their names are Pat Goltz and Cathy Callaghan, and as members of the Columbus, Ohio, chapter of NOW, they came forward with their pro-life views. They were told by NOW's leadership that they were forbidden from discussing abortion with any NOW members at any time or any place. So when Pat and Cathy, of course, continued to discuss it, they were expelled from the organization. The two women went on to found Feminists for Life of America, and I'm happy to report that we've just finished celebrating our 25th anniversary together.

So why *should* we care what some "humorless old biddies" from the nineteenth century had to say about abortion? Indeed, one might just as well ask, "Why even commemorate the accomplishments of these brave pioneer women in the first place?" I think the answer is rather simple: Without a firm understanding of where we've come from, it's difficult to have a clear vision of where we need to go. And I think on no other contemporary issue is this more true than on the abortion issue, which mainstream feminist groups have made the very cornerstone of women's rights today.

Why *should* we care that, in 1873, Elizabeth Cady Stanton wrote about abortion: "When we consider that women are treated as property, it is degrading for women to treat their children as property, to be disposed of as they see fit?" [See footnote on letter 34.] The answer is evident. We've long rejected the notion that a woman is the property of her husband or that her worth is dependent on whether she is wanted by a man. It is the height of hypocrisy to turn around and impose the same unjust standards on our children. Indeed, when we take any individual and base their worth on someone else's emotional reaction to them, we are rationalizing prejudice. "It's a baby if I want it; it's a fetus if I don't." Throughout history we've seen how such dehumanizing rhetoric has been used to deny dignity and basic human rights to other oppressed groups, be they women, minorities, gays, Jews, the disabled, the unborn.

It's no surprise then that many of the founders of the American feminist movement were also abolitionists, children's rights advocates, and activists in the peace movement. They unanimously rejected abortion, not because the procedure was less safe at the time but because they considered it to be "child murder"—that's what it was called in Susan B. Anthony's newspaper *The Revolution*. The early feminists opposed abortion primarily because it took a human life. They knew then, as now, that killing is not a legitimate solution to conflict, particularly when nonlethal alternatives exist. They knew then, as we know now, that violence—which reflects traditional masculine aggression—solves nothing, that it only begets more violence and often ends up hurting the perpetrator as much as the victim. They knew then, as we know now, that abortion is not a woman's right, but rather a grievous wrong against her.

Why *should* we care that, in 1875, the flamboyant free-love advocate and first woman to run for president, Victoria Woodhull, wrote, "Every woman knows that if she were free, she would never bear an unwished-for child, nor think of murdering one before its birth." Why? Because most women don't abort out of freedom of choice but out of a sense that they have no other choices. And as long as we are giving in to abortion 1.3 million times a year, we have relieved society of its obligation to meet the real needs of women: affordable day care, flexible work and school schedules, comprehensive health care, attractive adoption options, increased male sexual responsibility. These are the things that can liberate women—abortion will not. By advocating abortion instead of working for social changes that would make it easier to combine children and career, we have hindered progress in achieving our legitimate goals.

Why *should* it concern us that, in 1869, Mattie Brinkerhoff wrote, "When a man steals to satisfy hunger, we may safely conclude that there is something wrong in society. So when a woman destroys the life of her unborn child, it is evidence that either by education or circumstances, she has been greatly wronged"? Why? Because if we truly valued women and their reproductive capacities, we would *never* force them to choose between their life goals and their offspring just to fit into a society dominated by men. Nor would we define such an abhorrent choice as "liberating."

Our foremothers knew, as we know now, that if, in order to be equal, women have to resort to domination and violence to become like men—wombless and unpregnant at will—then we have not established justice.

As feminist writer Daphne de Jong put it, we have "simply adopted the standards of our oppressor and fashioned ourselves in his image."

I think we *should* care that Alice Paul, author of the original ERA of 1923, told a colleague that abortion is "the ultimate exploitation of woman." Abortion promotes a playboy mentality that regards women as sex "objects," which, if broken by pregnancy, can be "fixed" by abortion, only to be used and used again. Rather than liberating women, abortion liberates men from obligations to their partners and their children. "Abortion is the ultimate exploitation of woman."

Not every woman need be a mother. But when we regard the uniquely female power, beauty, and strength of pregnancy as a disease or deviation, we are internalizing attitudes of low self-esteem toward our own bodies. Consider former *Time* Magazine White House correspondent Nina Burleigh's recent comments in the *Washington Post* that she would gladly have had oral sex with President Clinton just to thank him for keeping abortion legal. "Abortion is the ultimate exploitation of woman."

We can see from these and so many examples how deep the roots of sexism truly run in our culture. And while much progress has been made in the last 150 years, we still have a long way to go.

As the visionary leader Susan B. Anthony said about abortion in 1869, "We want prevention, not merely punishment. We must reach the root of the evil.… It is practiced by those whose inmost souls revolt from the dreadful deed." Instead of embracing abortion as a fundamental right, we need to work to eradicate it by reaching the root cause—the oppression and sexual exploitation of women—that enable abortions to flourish.

As the feminist movement continues on our path to equality into the next century, let us honor our foremothers by paying them the ultimate compliment: Listen to them. Let us honor our sisters by confronting our failures and working through them together as a sign of deep commitment and love. Let us honor our daughters, both born and unborn, by modeling our values, by embracing causes that reflect not domination and violence, but true feminist ideals of justice and equality, causes that will advance our legitimate goals and actually bring women the respect we deserve. *Then* we can declare in full confidence that feminism is *not* dead, that failure *is* impossible, and finally that peace does *indeed* begin in the womb. Thank you.

INDEX

(Entries Organized by Letter or Article Number)